The Struggle across
the Taiwan Strait

The Struggle across the Taiwan Strait

The Divided China Problem

Ramon H. Myers
and Jialin Zhang

HOOVER INSTITUTION PRESS
Stanford University   Stanford, California

www.hoover.org

Hoover Institution Press Publication No. 542

First printing, 2006
13   12   11   10   09   08   07   06   9   8   7   6   5   4   3   2   1

Manufactured in the United States of America

The paper used in this publication meets the minimum requirements of the American National Standard for Information Sciences—Permanence of Paper for Printed Library Materials, ANSI Z39.48-1992. ⊚

Library of Congress Cataloging-in-Publication Data
Myers, Ramon Hawley, 1929–
    The struggle across the Taiwan strait : the divided China problem / by Ramon H. Myers and Jialin Zhang
        p.   cm. — (Hoover Institution Press publication, 542)
    ISBN 0-8179-4692-6 (alk. paper)
    1. Taiwan—Relations—China.   2. China—Relations—Taiwan.   3. Chinese reunification question, 1949–   I. Title: Divided mainland China–Taiwan problem.   II. Zhang, Jialin, 1933–
III. Title.   IV. Series.
DS799.63.C6M94   2006
327.5105124'909—dc22   2005027995

*In memory of Wang Daohan,
chairman of the Association for
Relations across the Taiwan Strait,
and Koo Chen-fu, chairman of
the Strait Exchange Foundation,
for their great efforts toward peacefully
resolving the divided China problem.*

Contents

Introduction

This short, concise history aims to inform readers on how China divided, in 1949, into two regimes that have struggled ever since to achieve political goals that have become increasingly incompatible.

The protagonists of this continuing struggle are as follows. The regime we denote as the mainland China authorities has controlled the territories of the People's Republic of China from October 1, 1949, to the present, and its leaders have always insisted that Taiwan and its offshore island must eventually be unified with their regime, by war if need be, but preferably by peaceful means.

The regime we call the Taiwan or Republic of China authorities has controlled Taiwan, the Pescadores, and certain offshore islands ever since the Nationalist Government reclaimed those territories from Japan on October 25, 1945.

Our narrative describes how, for more than a half century, these competing authorities struggled to unify China, until a political earthquake shook Taiwan on March 18, 2000. Taiwan's people had elected a new political regime, which then began changing the political rules by which the former Guomindang (GMD, or Chinese National People's Party) regime had struggled with the mainland regime to unify China. In essence, this newly elected Taiwan regime championed a new belief system that not only intensified the struggle with the mainland Chinese authorities but locked both sides into a new contest that increased the probability of war rather than peace.

We refer to the 'one China principle,' 'Taiwan is a part of China,' etc., as terms conveying the sentiments and beliefs expressed in these competing political regimes. Our story becomes complex after the March 18, 2000, election when Taiwan's society became more divided between groups supporting independence from China, groups supporting unification of China, and groups wanting no change from the status quo. Taiwan's political parties have also advanced different arguments as to how Taiwan should evolve. Never have the island's people been so divided about their future and priorities. So far, the groups in this debate lack the evidence needed to be persuasive. As the English philosopher Bertrand Russell once put it, "The most savage controversies are those about matters as to which there is no good evidence either way."

This new struggle within Taiwan and between Taiwan and mainland China is now influenced by a new belief system we call "Taiwan nationalism." This term denotes a shared ideology of strong identification with the territory of Taiwan, a shared history of social and political change in which Taiwan was controlled by different agents from outside, and shared symbols signifying the primacy of Taiwan's distinctive culture. The ideology of Taiwan nationalism also includes the claim that "Taiwan is separate from China and already is a sovereign, democratic nation." As for those believing in Taiwan nationalism, if they also believe Taiwan should be politically separate (independent) from China, we refer to them as Taiwan nationalists and separatists.

Some in the Democratic Progressive Party (DPP) embrace the belief system of Taiwan nationalism and separatism, but many in both the DPP and GMD-led coalitions simply advocate the ideology of "Taiwan nationalism" because they only want to reform the political system and differentiate Taiwan as democratic and sovereign. While still advocating Taiwan's political status quo, they also want to engage the mainland China regime. If conditions were to improve in cross strait relations, more might consider forming a China Commonwealth or China Federation in which Taiwan would still be a sovereign nation, yet part of China.

The mainland Chinese authorities strongly oppose those groups supportive of Taiwan nationalism and separatism, and have threatened to use force to prevent Taiwan from leaving the orbit of China.

These clashing beliefs take place within the Asia-Pacific region, a region of enormous wealth, high population density, and rapid change. As tensions across the Taiwan Strait worsened after 2000, discussions about possible war between the two sides became more frequent. Such a conflict would likely spread, disrupt the region's prosperity, and possibly produce long term chaos. Taiwan's democracy still offers the people the hope that the leaders of these two regimes will realize that using force, rather than reason and restraint, is too high a price for ending the Chinese civil war begun more than a half century ago.

1. China Divides into Two Rival Regimes

In autumn 1945, communist forces moved into Manchuria and obtained superior weapons from the Soviets, who had been there since August. The Chinese Communist Party (CCP) troops occupied vast parts of the countryside by imposing land reform and establishing their village and township governance. By using Mao's strategy of encircling the cities and isolating them from the countryside, CCP troops, now in possession of better military equipment, soon defeated the American-trained Nationalist forces and advanced southward into North China.[1] By January 31, 1949, Communist troops had occupied Beijing, and on October 1, 1949, Chairman Mao stood at Tiananmen to proclaim the founding of a new Chinese state, the People's Republic of China.[2]

Despite many hundreds of millions of dollars in U.S. military and economic aid given to Nationalist China between 1945 and 1949, the Guomindang (GMD)-led Nationalist government never

1. Steven I. Levine, "Mobilizing for War: Rural Revolution in Manchuria as an Instrument for War," in Kathleen Hartford and Steven M. Goldstein, eds., *Single Sparks: China's Rural Revolutions* (Armonk, N.Y.: M. E. Sharpe, 1989), pp. 151–75. Also Steven I. Levine, *Anvil of Victory: The Communist Revolution in Manchuria, 1945–1948* (New York: Columbia University Press, 1987).

2. Zhonggong Zhongyang Wenxian Yanjiushi (The research section on materials of the Communist Party's central headquarters), *Jianguo yilai Mao Zedong wengao* (The writings of Mao Zedong since the founding of the People's Republic of China) (Beijing: Zhongyang wenxuan chubanshe, 1979), pp. 14–15.

provided the leadership, the tactics, or the official and civil organizations necessary to win the civil war. Declining morale and
mounting corruption also weakened Nationalist leadership, and
within a year the CCP-led military forces were able to defeat the
Nationalist government in a series of battles in North, Central,
and South China.

By early 1950 the new communist government had unified
the China mainland and begun military preparations for invading
Taiwan, where the Nationalist leader, President Chiang Kai-shek,
and his son, Chiang Ching-kuo, had taken refuge on May 25,
1949. Father and son, along with remnants of the GMD and
Nationalist government, vowed to make Taiwan their last-ditch
stand. On July 14, father and son flew first to Canton and then
to the Southwest (where the Nationalist government had relo-
cated in 1938 to resist Japan), hoping to build a guerrilla base to
resist the CCP. But they found no popular support for their cause
because the local people and elites, remembering the years of
oppressive, corrupt Nationalist government rule, had decided to
welcome the new communist regime. Taiwan was now Chiang
Kai-shek's last hope. But why Taiwan?

When President Chiang and his son arrived in Taiwan on
May 25, 1949, Taiwan was their last hope of refuge, but a majority
of the island's people did not admire the Nationalists. President
Chiang began rebuilding the island's administration, reorganizing
the GMD, preparing the island's defenses, and hoping for a miracle. On January 5, 1950, expecting the island to fall soon into
communist hands, President Harry Truman stated that "the
United States will not provide military aid or advice to Chinese
forces on Formosa." His secretary of state, Dean Acheson, on that
same day had this to say: "The President says, we are not going
to use our forces in connection with the present situation in Formosa. We are not going to attempt to seize the island. We are
not going to get involved militarily in any way on the island of

Formosa."[3] All signs indicated that the United States had finally washed its hands of the Chiang regime and that civil war soon would end, leading to China's reunification.

But some six months later, on June 25, 1950, North Korean armor and infantry slammed deep inside South Korea. President Truman and his advisers immediately reassessed the intentions of the Soviet Union and communist-ruled North Korea. They concluded that "the occupation of Formosa by Communist forces would be a direct threat to the security of the Pacific Area and to United States forces performing their lawful and necessary functions in that area."[4] Thus, on June 27, President Truman informed the United States and the world that "I have ordered the Seventh Fleet to prevent any attack on Formosa. As a corollary of this action, I am calling upon the Chinese government of Formosa to cease all air and sea operations against the mainland."[5]

The United States decided to restrain both Chinese regimes from going to war. The two political parties that had contested each other in China's long civil war governed separate territories, divided by the Taiwan Strait. These two Chinese regimes would continue their struggle but in different ways. The United States still had not been able to extricate itself from China's civil war.

In fact, it was U.S. naval and air power intervention in the Taiwan Strait that created the divided China problem of today. A crucial legacy of U.S. intervention was that the PRC leaders believed that the United States had cheated them of a historical opportunity to unify the country. In their hearts they vowed never to allow foreign intervention to obstruct China's reunification. For that reason, American leaders should heed Beijing's warning that it intends to unify China, whether by peaceful means or by force.

Although China divided after 1949 to become the PRC in Bei-

3. Hungdah Chiu, *China and the Question of Taiwan*, pp. 221–22.
4. Ibid., p. 228.
5. Ibid.

jing and ROC in Taipei, it only superficially resembles the two
Germanys, the two Koreas, and the two Vietnams after World
War II. Many Taiwanese politicians and scholars have used this
resemblance to contend that Taiwan is an independent, sovereign
state. Taiwan's authorities asserted in February 1997, in a government report titled *"The Issue of 'one China' in Perspective,"* the
following:

> China has been in a divided status since the Chinese Com-
> munist regime was founded in 1949. Because neither Taipei
> nor Beijing has ruled the other side, neither side can repre-
> sent the other. Therefore, neither side can claim that it rep-
> resents the whole China, and it can represent only the part
> over which it exerts effective control. Thus, there is a "divided
> China," not a "one China."[6]

According to this interpretation, mainland and Taiwan are two
sovereign states. But Beijing has a different interpretation, and
claims that the divided China is not another divided Korea, or
formerly divided Germany and Vietnam for the following reasons.

First, the division of Germany originated from fascism's defeat
in World War II and by international agreements between the
winners. The same scenario applied to Korea and Vietnam, first
occupied by the winning powers, then divided by regional wars
and international agreements. China's division arose from its long
history of civil war and the U.S. involvement in that struggle. That
change in political power and sovereignty was produced by a continuing civil war that has never been terminated by any formal
agreement.

Second, unlike the former two Germanies and today's two
Koreas that later achieved cross-recognition and were admitted
to the UN and other international organizations, the PRC ultimately inherited almost all domestic and international legal rights

6. *Central Daily*, Taipei, February 23, 1997.

of the former ROC by negotiating normal relations with other countries.

Third, the former divided parts of Germany, Korea and Vietnam were roughly equal in size, population and economic potential. Not so for the divided China. In mainland China, the Communist forces seized more than 99 percent of the country, with more than 98 percent of the population. Therefore, although China was divided over the last 50 odd years, this separation can be called a partial or quasi-division.

Finally, and perhaps most important, the Chinese civil war has not legally been concluded, and both PRC and ROC Constitutions still claim the mainland and Taiwan as part of their territory. For these reasons, the divided China problem is a special case that has evolved in a complex historical context.[7]

The Two Regimes Continue Their Struggle

Furious that American military power had been sent to the Taiwan Strait to prevent PRC forces from occupying Taiwan, Mao Zedong and his minister of foreign affairs, Zhou Enlai, denounced such intervention in China's civil war. The PRC also appealed to the United Nations, without success, to condemn American intervention in China's internal affairs. Chinese resentment of American actions to protect Taiwan likely emboldened the PRC's decision to enter the Korean War.

In response, the United States began building alliances in the Asia-Pacific region to contain the spread of communism. On April 18, 1952, the United States arranged for the ROC and Japan to sign a peace treaty; on December 21, 1954, the U.S. and ROC

---

7. See Liu Hong, "On the Evolution of the Major Contradictions Between the Two sides of the Strait," *Taiwan Studies*, Beijing, No.3, 1997, pp. 6–11; and Wang Sheng, "The Knot and its Untying of 'one China,'" *Taiwan Studies*, Beijing, No.1, 1998, pp. 22–27.

governments signed a mutual defense treaty.[8] In a similar way the United States gradually cobbled together a series of alliances with Japan, South Korea, Taiwan, the Philippines, Australia and New Zealand, and even some Southeast Asian states, to contain Communist China.

Meanwhile, the two Chinese regimes began building the societies their respective political parties advocated as best for China and its people. The CCP, by imposing its power on urban elites and extending its control to the villages, swiftly began to replace the market economy with a socialist-type command economy, extolled the Marxist and Maoist ideologies as *the* doctrines of truth for the Chinese people, and organized a cooperative-type society by merging the workplace and family household.

Having imposed martial law in July 1949, in 1950 Taiwan's GMD-led authoritarian government initiated local elections in which "limited democracy" gradually evolved under single-party rule, along with a state-guided, highly productive market economy. By limited democracy we mean elections for local government officials and members of the Taiwan Provincial Government Assembly but not the provincial governor, the central government's president and vice-president, and National Assembly members.

Confucianism, Western liberalism, and Sun Yat-sen's doctrine competed for popular support, and family households had a high degree of freedom of choice. By 1960, the two Chinese societies were diverging along different development paths. The mainland regime exerted almost total control over society, whereas the Taiwan regime allowed for a society having greater freedom, but crushed any criticism or activities challenging its legitimacy.

Meanwhile, the civil war continued but in a different form of

8. Ibid., pp. 245–46 and pp. 250–52.

struggle. The ROC government's policy toward the mainland during Chiang Kai-shek and Chiang Ching-kuo's early years of rule was "counterattacking the mainland, recovering the whole Chinese territory (*fan gong fu guo*)," and using its "Three People's Principles of Nationalism, Democracy, and Social Welfare" (*san min zhuyi*) to unify China. While pushing economic and social reconstruction in Taiwan, Chiang's government used U.S. military assistance to foment insurrection against the communist regime, in an attempt to restore the ROC's rule in the mainland.

In 1952 and 1953, when the Korean War raged, the Nationalist government cooperated with American CIA units to launch guerrilla attacks on communist-held offshore islands across from Taiwan for the purpose of diverting Chinese troops from the Korean War to Southeast China.[9] But the U.S. government soon aborted the operation and devoted its attention to preventing the ROC government from carrying out any military activities against the mainland or any covert operations in western and southwestern China.[10] Meanwhile the U.S. 7th fleet patrolled the Taiwan Strait to prevent either side from attacking the other.

Both regimes also nurtured Chinese nationalism to arouse the public's enthusiasm for reunifying China. In the summer of 1953, when the Korean War ended, the PRC leadership realized it had no national policy to mobilize popular sentiment for resolving the Taiwan problem. In June 1954 Mao Zedong informed Zhou Enlai, then in Geneva brokering a peace between the communist Viet Minh and France, that "we were wrong not to press for the lib-

---

9. The CIA covert operations directed against the offshore islands of Fujian province have been described in Frank Holober, *Raiders of the China Coast* (Annapolis, Md.: Naval Institute Press, 1999).

10. For the best account of America's efforts to rein in the ROC government from provocative military ventures in mainland China, see Steven M. Goldstein, "The United States and Taiwan, 1949–1998: The Sometime Allies," in Michel Oksenberg, ed., *American Security Relations in the Pacific: Past, Present, and the Future* (Stanford: Stanford University Press, forthcoming).

eration of Taiwan immediately after the conclusion of the Korean War. If we do not do that now, we will repeat the same political mistake."[11]

On July 23, 1954, the *People's Daily* announced that "we must definitely liberate Taiwan."[12] Throughout mainland China, CCP cadres began holding discussion meetings to whip up enthusiasm for the PRC to recover Taiwan while hoisting banners that proclaimed "We must definitely liberate Taiwan."[13] To ensure the public's commitment to achieve the nation's goal of "liberating Taiwan," the PRC regime inserted that message into textbooks, conducted study sessions for party cadres, and made frequent public statements to that effect.

Contained and isolated by the U.S. and its allies in the 1950s, the PRC had no channel to express its attitude on the Taiwan issue to the international community. It was excluded from the UN, and had diplomatic relations with only 20 countries, among them 10 belonging to the socialist bloc. Failing to find a better option, the PRC used a strategy of focused military threat.[14] In 1954, and again in 1958, the government ordered the extensive shelling of the offshore island of Jinmen (and not other ROC claimed islands) to convince the Chinese people on both sides of the Taiwan Strait and the international community of the PRC's serious intention to recover Taiwan, but not initiate any armed conflict at that time.

---

11. Zhang Zanhe, *Liangan guanxi bianjianshi* (A history of the changing circumstances regarding cross-Strait relations) (Taiwan: Zhouzhi wenhua shiye gufen yu gongsi, 1996), pp. 119–20.

12. "Yi yi jiefang Taiwan" (We definitely must liberate Taiwan), *Renmin ribao* (People's Daily), July 23, 1954, p. 1.

13. Michel Leiris, *Journal de Chine* (China diary) (Paris: Gallimard, 1994), p. 50.

14. He Zhongshan: "The Evolution From 'Liberating Taiwan' Toward 'Peaceful Reunification,'" *Hundred Year Tide*, No.10, 2002, p. 32.

The 1958 shelling influenced subsequent cross-strait as well as U.S.-China relations. On August 23, 1958, The Liberation Army launched more than 20,000 shells onto Jinmen island, and successfully blockaded it. Taiwan's Nationalist troops incurred heavy damage. This event promptly drew the attention of the U.S. and other East Asian countries. The U.S. government, while condemning the PRC's "armed aggression," strengthened its naval and air force buildup in the Taiwan Strait, convoyed Taiwan's supply fleet and rendered other military assistance. But, the U.S. also expressed its reluctance to be drawn into the crisis. John Foster Dulles, the U.S. Secretary of State, stated on September 30, 1958, that it was not sensible and prudent for Taiwan to station so many forces in Jinmen and Mazu, and said, "We (the U.S.) don't have any legal obligations to defend the off-shore islands."[15] The U.S. Congress and the public also urged the administration to give up Jinmen and Mazu. Beijing interpreted this U.S. stance as a deal to give up Jinmen and Mazu in return for Beijing's armistice and no use of force, thus establishing a demarcation line in the middle of the Taiwan Strait and perpetuating the division of China.[16]

President Chiang also resented the Dulles statement, and he reiterated that Jinmen and Mazu are inalienable territories of the ROC and will never be given up. Sensing discord between Chiang and the U.S. over the Jinmen and Mazu issue, Mao Zedong concluded that having the two islands in the Nationalist troop's hands was in the best interest of preserving one China and avoiding U.S. intervention. The Beijing government declared that it

15. Su Ge, "Paoji Jinmen di Juece Ji Qi Yinxian, (Decision-Making of Shelling Jinmen and its Effects)," *Zhonggong Danshi Zhiliao (Historical References of CCP)*, Vol, 66, 1998, Party History Publishing House, Beijing, p.126.
16. See He Zhongshan, p. 34.

would only sporadically shell Jinmen to induce Nationalist troops to defend it.[17]

For Beijing and Taipei as well, the shelling of Jinmen demonstrated a tacit understanding between Taipei and Beijing to oppose any U.S. "two Chinas" policy. Since then, both sides have readjusted their policies toward each other. Beijing shifted its Taiwan policy from military confrontation to political confrontation, while Taiwan soon abandoned "counterattacking the mainland" and concentrated upon developing Taiwan's economy and society while hoping that contradictions within the PRC would bring about its collapse.

On May 22, 1960, the CCP's Politbureau approved new guidelines on Taiwan policy: It is better to leave Taiwan in the hands of the Chiangs (father and son) rather than in the hands of the Americans; Beijing can wait to see what the Chiangs will do, and liberating Taiwan can be completed by the next generation, not necessarily by this generation. Chairman Mao Zedong further stated, "We will allow Taiwan to retain its own social system and institutions." Later, Zhou Enlai advanced a general principle for unification called the "one key link and four outlines." The 'one key link' meant "Taiwan should be integrated with China." The 'four outlines' were: (1), all military and political power and personnel designations, except diplomatic affairs that belong to the central government, are at the Chiangs discretion; (2), the shortfalls in military and civil budgets are to be covered by the central government; (3), social reforms in Taiwan can be postponed until conditions permit and with the consent of the Chiangs; (4), both sides will not send agents to the other side to sabotage unity.[18] The Beijing leadership already was considering how to integrate Taiwan with the mainland.

---

17. Ibid.
18. Legislative Affairs Commission of the Standing Committee of the

On Taiwan, the ROC regime also used nationalism to mobilize the populace to oppose communism, in order to recover the mainland and reunify China. Under the banner of preserving Chinese civilization, the regime produced textbooks and propaganda materials emphasizing that Taiwan had always been part of China. The authorities prepared primary schoolbooks that taught the national language or Beijing dialect and stressed Chinese history, geography, literature, and Confucian ethics. At the same time the authorities discouraged using the Taiwan dialect and rarely mentioned Taiwan's experience under Japanese colonial rule.

Chiang Kai-shek, and later his son Chiang Ching-kuo, always insisted upon a "One China" policy and the sovereign legitimacy of the ROC. They opposed any attempt to promote Taiwan independence and the "undetermining of Taiwan's status." The authorities had strongly suppressed an urban uprising in early 1947 whose leaders had demanded greater self-rule. They also declared martial law in 1949 and then relentlessly repressed dissidents, including an embryonic Taiwan independence movement that had formed after the February 28, 1947 uprising. Overall, fiercely hostile as Chiang's regime's policy was toward the mainland, the Taiwan authorities managed cross-strait relations under the shadow of the continuing civil war while insisting on upholding its "One China principle." The ROC still claimed it represented mainland China, Taiwan, and the offshore islands.

Each regime also continued to claim sovereignty over a "One China" that included Taiwan. The PRC Constitution's preamble proclaimed that "Taiwan is part of the sacred territory of the People's Republic of China. It is the inviolable duty of all Chinese people, including our compatriots in Taiwan, to accomplish the

---

National People's Congress, *Constitution of the People's Republic of China* (Beijing: Foreign Language Press, 1994), p. 5.

great task of reunifying the motherland."[19] The ROC regime used its 1947 Constitution, approved by the National Assembly in that same year, to claim that the 1911 "existing national boundaries shall not be altered except by resolution of the National Assembly."[20] A majority of the National Assembly elected in 1947 had found refuge in Taiwan, where they not only routinely voted every six years to elect the ROC's president and vice president but also held the political power to revise the ROC Constitution.

Each regime competed for diplomatic recognition and entry into international organizations such as the United Nations. Neither regime offered dual diplomatic relations with another country that had established diplomatic ties with the other. Between 1954 and 1969 the ROC regime, with American support, increased its diplomatic ties with other nations from thirty-nine to sixty-nine, securing recognition from the many new nations established in those years. Meanwhile, from 1965 to 1969 the PRC regime's friendly states declined from forty-eight to forty-four, largely because of concern over the Great Cultural Revolution that swept China in those years. The United States had managed to retain the ROC's original seat for China in the U.N Security Council and even mustered member support each year to prevent the PRC from gaining entry into that body. But after 1969 the tide shifted, and in 1971 a new majority of U.N members approved that the PRC replace the ROC in the Security Council.

For three decades the two Chinese regimes had been adversaries, competing in every possible way to project their influence in the world. In order to win international support for their claim of representing "One China," each used any means that could be

---

19. Legislative Affairs Commission of the Standing Committee of the National People's Congress, *Constitution of the People's Republic of China* (Beijing: Foreign Language Press, 1994), p. 5.

20. Government Information Office, *Republic of China, 1999: The Republic of China Yearbook* (Taipei: Government Information Office, 1999), p. 679.

exploited to gain an advantage over the other. Both regimes remained committed to the reunification of China, yet each developed a different system of governance, economy, and society. The struggle between the two regimes in these three decades was based upon which regime could enhance its legitimacy by representing "One China" in the international community. The civil war merely continued in a different form of struggle.

2. The Move toward Détente

The death of Chairman Mao Zedong in September 1976 created a leadership vacuum that was soon filled by Deng Xiaoping, the CCP's most original mind and politician par excellence. Deng accurately sensed the people's alienation from the party and state and was aware of the enormous waste and inefficiency of the Maoist command economy that had brought the country to a state of near exhaustion and ruin. Deng formulated a compelling vision for China's people: To make China powerful and prosperous, they would work to raise its productive powers instead of engaging in divisive "class struggle," and to that end, the state and party would initiate reforms to open up the country to the outside world. Emboldened by having loosened ties between the United States and the ROC regime in 1972, Beijing's leaders decided on a new approach toward the divided China problem. They would propose that Taipei's leaders embark on peaceful negotiations to agree upon a new formula, a novel concept of federation, for ending the division of China.

Beijing's Policy Toward Taiwan

In late 1978, for the first time since China divided, Beijing's leaders adopted a new attitude toward their old enemy. They stated that the people of Taiwan and mainland "are all from the same ancestors, and we are all one family. We share a common position by which we can reach an understanding based upon consensus (*gongshi*), and we should develop three channels (*santong*) for communications and find four ways for exchange (*siliu*)."[1] Beijing then offered Taipei some concrete proposals to bring these developments about.

On January 1, 1979, the Standing Committee of the Fifth National People's Congress issued "A Message to Taiwan Compatriots" calling for negotiations to achieve China's reunification. Then on January 30, Deng Xiaoping told the U.S. Congress, "We no longer use the phrase 'liberate Taiwan'; so long as Taiwan returns to the Motherland, we will respect the reality and the existing system there."[2] On September 30, 1981, Marshall Ye Jianying, chairman of the National People's Congress, issued a nine-point proposal calling for negotiations between the CCP and GMD, expanding people-to-people exchanges, promising Taiwan a high degree of autonomy after reunification, and guaranteeing that Taiwan's way of life would not be changed. On January 26, 1983, Deng advanced a six-point policy based on the new formula that China could be reunified as "one country having two systems." That formula was later spelled out by Deng to mean that, after reunification, Taiwan would have a high degree of autonomy as a part of China; it could be called China-Taiwan, have a special flag, and preserve its constitution, military forces, system of government, and way of life. Moreover, no mainland troops would be dispatched to Taiwan, and the PRC government would never interfere with Taiwan's special status as part of China.[3]

As Beijing's leaders mounted their peace offensive against the Taiwan authorities, on January 1, 1979 they also normalized dip-

1. Zhang Zanhe, *Liangan guanxi bianjianshi*, pp. 254–55.

2. Jun Zhan, *Ending the Chinese Civil War: Power, Commerce and Conciliation between Beijing and Taipei* (New York: St. Martin's Press, 1993), p. 32.

3. Ibid., pp. 32–34.

lomatic relations with the United States (see Appendix, document 2). This diplomatic breakthrough originated from the famous Shanghai Communiqué, signed by the PRC and U.S. governments on February 28, 1972 (see Appendix, document 1). By persuading U.S. leaders to accept the "one China" principle, Beijing's leaders further isolated the ROC in the international order.

On January 1, 1979, ROC premier Sun Yun-suan dismissed Beijing's peace initiatives as lies designed to reduce American support for Taiwan. He also said that "history tells us that those who believe Communist lies always have suffered a tragic fate."[4] Premier Sun challenged the PRC regime to show its sincerity by respecting human rights, discarding Marxism, eliminating the CCP dictatorship, and abolishing communism.

On April 4, 1979, President Chiang Ching-kuo announced that the ROC government would adopt the principle of "three no's (*sanbu*)," which meant the ROC would have *no* negotiations, *no* communications, and *no* compromise with the PRC regime. Second, the ROC government intended to promote the peaceful transfer to the PRC regime of Sun Yat-sen's three principles of the people—the doctrine that had guided GMD policymaking on Taiwan—so that China eventually could be unified under a single belief system.[5] President Chiang was unable to present a blueprint for how that transfer should take place. The ROC regime, clearly on the defensive, was groping for a strategy to counter the PRC's "peace" initiatives.

President Chiang Ching-kuo Responds

Meanwhile, new developments were taking place behind the scenes. Taiwanese businesspersons began traveling through Hong Kong to China on special permits issued by the PRC regime,

4. Zhang Zenhe, *Liangan guanxi bianjianshi*, p. 258.
5. Ibid., p. 278.

and indirect trade between the two regimes rose rapidly. Between 1979 and 1985, total trade between the two regimes rose from $US 77 million to $US 1.1 billion, or more than twelve times in nominal terms.[6] More informal contacts between journalists, intrepid tourists, and fishermen took place, and contacts between sports people, academics, and students also increased. Although rarely mentioned, these exchanges had rapidly expanded by the mid-1980s. They could not have occurred without the tacit approval of the Chiang regime, and the extent of these contacts was remarkable.

In 1981 the PRC had established at least fourteen Taiwan Fishermen Reception Stations located in the provinces of Zhejiang, Fujian, and Guangdong, and in that same year, three thousand Taiwanese fishermen and four hundred fishing boats sought shelter in these stations.[7] Although previously, mainland fishermen had rarely entered Taiwan's harbors, after the ROC regime lifted martial law on July 15, 1987, their numbers rose, leading to a brisk two-way traffic of fishing boats visiting each side's harbors.

Another contact between the two regimes involved their agreeing, in March 1981, to participate in future Olympic Games,[8] a triumph of pragmatism over passionately held principles. The PRC agreed to be designated the "Chinese Olympic Committee (using its flag and national anthem), and the ROC agreed to be named the "Chinese Taipei Olympic Committee," with its anthem and flag being different from those presently used. Taipei agreed to change the name, flag, and anthem to participate in future Olympic Games, and the PRC gained entry into the Olympics.

Still another example of contact was the Asian Development Bank (ADB) issue. The ROC, a founding member of the ADB,

6. Hsin-Hsing Wu, *Bridging the Strait: Taiwan, China, and the Prospects for Reunification* (Hong Kong: Oxford University Press, 1994), p. 176.

7. Ibid., p. 161.

8. Ibid., pp. 180–81.

faced a challenge in 1983 when the PRC applied for ADB membership and insisted that the ROC be expelled. In May 1985, Beijing changed its position, stating that the PRC should be admitted as sole representative of China, whereas the ROC could remain as 'Taiwan, China,' or 'Taipei, China.' The United States and other ADB members had previously insisted that the PRC be admitted only if it agreed not to demand that the ROC be expelled, and for that reason, the PRC accepted the compromise. President Ronald Reagan even sent his national security adviser, William Clark, to Taipei to press the ROC to accept; on March 10, 1986, the ADB admitted the PRC, and the ROC stayed in ADB as 'Taipei, China.'[9] Both regimes had made concessions to ensure that their international financial policies would still be performed under the principle of "One China."

Then on May 3, 1986, a pilot flying an ROC China Airline (CAL) 747 Boeing cargo plane hijacked the plane to the PRC.[10] The ROC regime wanted CAL to negotiate with the PRC through a third party for the return of the plane. Beijing responded by asking CAL to send a representative to Beijing. CAL countered by urging that Hong Kong's Cathay Pacific Airways handle the problem in Hong Kong. From May 17 to 20, 1986, a CAL representative and a Beijing representative from the Civil Aviation Administration Bureau met in Hong Kong and reached an agreement to return the plane, cargo, and crew to Taiwan.

Finally, on October 15, 1987, the ROC's Executive Yuan passed a law, strongly encouraged by President Chiang Ching-kuo, that permitted retired ROC military personnel to visit mainland China to see their relatives. This arrangement, organized through the International Red Cross, was welcomed by the PRC, and soon after the ROC reciprocated by welcoming PRC military personnel visiting their relatives in Taiwan.

9. Ibid., pp. 186–87.
10. Ibid., pp. 192–92.

These many new contacts between the two Chinese regimes showed creative diplomacy and pragmatism as well as an awareness that cooperation, particularly through trade and investment, yielded mutual benefits. As a consequence of this change in behavior, by 1990, the total amount of trade between the two regimes had increased to US $4.0 billion, nearly a fourfold increase in nominal terms over that of 1985. But just as both regimes increased their contacts, on January 13, 1988, President Chiang died, signaling the passing of an era in Taiwan and the end of the Chiang family influence in political life.

After he had served nearly two years as acting president, in March 1990, the National Assembly elected Lee Teng-hui as the eighth Taiwanese president for a six-year term. Lee had narrowly defeated a bid by his party's conservative wing to elect its presidential (the Taiwanese Lin Yang-kang) and vice presidential (the mainlander Chiang Wei-kuo) favorites. The new president then began to replace the National Assembly with newly elected assembly members to revise the ROC Constitution, a huge step for promoting Taiwan's democratization.

Initially, when Chiang Ching-kuo designated Lee as successor, Lee was a staunch supporter of the "One China" policy. As one of Chiang's advisors recalled, when serving as governor of Taiwan Province in 1984, Lee responded to a question on his attitude toward "Taiwan independence," by emphatically saying that "China never discarded Taiwan in its history, how can Taiwan disassociate from China."[11] Chiang, happy with his statement and trusting Lee's loyalty to him and the GMD, two months later nominated Lee as vice president. When Lee became the president in 1988, he reaffirmed at his first press conference that

11. Chang Chu-yi, "My judgement of Chiang Ching-kuo's Nomination of Li Deng-hui as Vice-President," *Biographical Literature*, Vol. 47, No. 4, 1999, p.43.

"for the national policy of ROC, there is only a one-China policy, no two-China policies."[12]

On September 21, 1990, President Lee established the National Unification Council (NUC) to draft a new China policy.[13] The NUC did not include representatives of the main opposition party, the DPP, because the DPP refused to participate. Already, this new party, the DPP, had begun to champion Taiwan nationalism by publicly declaring in the 1987 local elections that Taiwan should be independent from China. Meanwhile, President Lee, who served as NUC chairman had set the agenda and invited persons of both genders, from the main professions and of different ethnic groups, to serve in the NUC.

On January 28, 1991, the NUC announced a new China policy that was embodied in its unification guidelines (see Appendix 5). These guidelines called for China's reunification in a three-phase process. In the first phase, both regimes would expand non-official, people-to-people contacts, renounce the use of force, respect the jurisdiction of each other's territories, and not deny the other's existence as a political entity. If these developments took place, the second phase would commence. Both regimes would then set up channels of official communications to establish direct postal, transportation, and commercial links across the Taiwan Strait. Officials of both sides could then visit each other. After these activities became routine, the third phase would begin by forming a bilateral consultative body to "jointly discuss the grand task of unification and map out a constitutional system to establish a democratic, free, and equitably, prosperous China."[14]

12. *Central Daily*, February 23, 1988.

13. For a good chronology of these events, see Winberg Chai, "Relations between the Chinese Mainland and Taiwan: Overview and Chronology," *Asian Affairs: An American Review* 26, no. 2 (summer 1999): 64–77.

14. See Guidelines for National Unification in Mainland Affairs Council, the Executive Yuan, the Republic of China, *MAC News Briefing*, Volume 1 (No. 0001No.0054) November 11, 1996–December 22, 1997 (Taipei: MAC).

On May 1, 1991, President Lee made another historic move. Backed by the National Assembly, he abolished the Temporary Articles passed in 1949 (which gave the office of the president enormous powers) and declared that the state of war between the two Chinese regimes was over. President Lee also vowed that Taiwan would never use military force to unify China. Lee hoped Beijing would respond by renouncing the use of force to unify China. Beijing's leaders did not do so.

Five months earlier, on January 18, 1991, the NUC and the office of the president had recommended that parliament (the Legislative Yuan) approve the establishment of a ministry under the Executive Yuan called the Mainland Affairs Council (MAC). The very next day the MAC approved the establishment of the Strait Exchange Foundation (SEF) to engage in periodic talks with the PRC regime. On December 16, 1991, the PRC regime established the Association for Relations Across the Taiwan Strait (ARATS) to talk with Taiwan's SEF. Both regimes had quickly moved to create the machinery for non-official contacts, discussions, and even formal agreements.

These new developments, coinciding with the deepening of Taiwan's democracy and growing Taiwanese nationalism, converged with the explosion of "China fever" across Taiwan, or expanding exchanges and growing trade across the Taiwan Strait. Not only had mainland China become the center for much attraction in Taiwan, but between 1987 and 1992, more than 4.2 million visits by people from Taiwan to the mainland took place, with about 40,000 mainlanders visiting Taiwan. Indirect trade between the two regimes was over US $10 billion, and Taiwan businesspersons had invested as much as US $10 billion in the PRC regime. Prior to 1992 little contact aside from fishing traffic had existed between the two sides. Something very new was taking place. A struggle of a new kind was about to begin.

The Emergence of a New Force
Opposing China's Unification

Despite these favorable trends, Taiwan specialists in the PRC regime worried about a new public debate that had arisen in Taiwan in the fall of 1989 and still continued: did the ROC regime's future lie with the unification of China or with being independent of China? This debate had first surfaced in September 1989, three months before Taiwan's local elections, when the DPP won a resounding election victory by capturing six of the twenty county/city positions, a first for the opposition party.[15] As Taiwan's elites passionately debated the issue of "independence" versus "reunification," public opinion polls showed that in late 1990 around 30 percent favored unification, only 2.9 percent supported independence, 25.0 percent wanted the status quo, and 22.2 percent held no opinion or could not respond.[16]

The public debate about Taiwan nationalism did not go ignored in Beijing. On June 7, 1991 the Taiwan Affairs Office of the CCP's Central Committee, responding to the debate in Taiwan as well as the ROC's unification guidelines, sternly warned that the PRC regime would not renounce the use of force against the ROC regime if (1) foreign forces interfered in China's reunification, and (2) elements in Taiwan tried to create "two Chinas," "one country, two governments," or "Taiwan independence." It concluded, "We will never sit by and watch Taiwan become 'independent.'"[17] Despite this grim warning, and the ROC regime's

15. Linda Chao and Ramon H. Myers, *The First Chinese Democracy: Political Life in the Republic of China on Taiwan* (Baltimore and London: Johns Hopkins University Press, 1998), p. 172.

16. See Gallup Organization, *Taiwan di qi minchong kan liangan jiaoliu minyi diaocha baogao* (A public opinion survey report on how the people of Taiwan area regard cross-strait exchanges) (Taipei: Gallup Organization, USA, 1990), p. 46.

17. Hungdah Chiu, "The Koo-Wang Talks and Intra-Chinese Relations," *American Journal of Chinese Studies* 2, no. 2 (October 1994): 226.

rejection of it, both sides approved establishing the SEF and the ARATS to facilitate cross-strait negotiations.[18]

Few, whether inside or outside of Taiwan, realized the implications that Taiwan's democratization would have on the longstanding divided China problem. Meanwhile, the U.S. Government had passed the Taiwan Relations Act (TRA), and this law committed the U.S. government to possible actions to guarantee a peaceful resolution of the divided China problem if the mainland China regime threatened to undermine regional peace and stability. (See Appendix, Document 3.) But the TRA stipulated no clear course of action for the U.S. government if Taiwan's democratically elected leaders decided to declare independence from mainland China or approve a national referendum to reject unification with China.

By establishing the TRA law the U.S. government had not extricated itself from the old Chinese civil war; instead it was now a new player in the ongoing struggle between the two Chinese regimes. If Taiwan's democracy deepened, Beijing's leaders might perceive that Taiwan's elected authorities posed a major obstacle to China's reunification. Such a political development would raise tensions across the Taiwan Strait and initiate an arms race. Few at the time perceived the following political nightmare.

As Taiwan's democracy advanced, Taiwan nationalism and separatism—the term we denote for a belief system in which people believe they are Taiwanese, not Chinese, and have no desire to unite with mainland China's people by any political system—could become a new force in Taiwan's political life and sorely divide Taiwan's people.

18. Hungdah Chiu, "The Koo-Wang Talks and Intra-Chinese Relations," *American Journal of Chinese Studies* 2, no. 2 (October 1994): 226.

3. Détente and Its Collapse

In March 1992, SEF and ARATS started negotiations to authenticate notarized documents and exchange "indirect" registered mail. No direct mail service was available at that time, and all mail had to be routed via Hong Kong. Prior to negotiations, however, ARATS demanded that mainland China's regime's "one China" principle be accepted as a prerequisite for dialogue. The SEF did not accept.

When negotiations resumed in Hong Kong on October 28, ARATS again demanded its "one China" principle be the *sine qua non* but agreed to let the SEF state its interpretation of "one China." Two days later, SEF responded to ARATS, emphasizing that both sides of the Taiwan Strait belong to "one China in which there exist two political entities on an equal footing"; both entities should "strive for a peaceful and democratic China." After more discussion both sides still could not agree on a mutual, satisfactory "one China" principle.

Later, SEF presented a modified proposal stating that "on both sides of the Taiwan Strait, by making common effort to achieve national unification, both adhere to the principle of 'one China'; but as for the meaning of "one China" each side can differ from the other to denote its meaning." SEF also recommended that both sides, based on what they now agreed, could orally state their positions on the issue. ARATS sent SEF a cable message on November 3, to "respect and accept" the recommendation, concurring that both sides would "define the principle of one China in an oral statement."

ARATS telephoned SEF about its oral statement as follows: "Both sides of the Strait adhere to the 'one China' principle in their effort to achieve the unification of the nation. But in the negotiations between the two sides on administrative affairs, the political meaning of 'one China' should not be mentioned."[1]

In response, SEF stated in a press release: "We (SEF) will express the concrete content of the oral statement (on one China) in line with the 'Guidelines for National Unification' and the resolution on 'one China' adopted by the National Unification Council on August 1 of this year (1992)." The "one China" resolution reads in part: ". . . Both sides of the Strait adhere to the principle of 'one China.' They each advanced different connotations [of 'one China'], however. The Chinese communist authorities regard 'one China' as the People's Republic of China, consider Taiwan after China's unification in the future to be a 'special administrative district' under its domain . . . [Our definition is:] 'One China' referred to hereinafter is the Republic of China that has existed to date since its founding in 1912 and whose sovereignty extends over all of China, albeit only Taiwan, Penghu, Kinmen and Matsu are now under its rule. Taiwan is a part of China. The mainland is also a part of China."[2]

As a matter of fact, Taipei and Beijing had agreed, prior to their negotiations in Hong Kong, that there is only one China. What they concurred in 1992 was their agreeing to disagree with each other on the definition of one China.

As we can see from both sides' oral statements, there was a consensus between the two sides regarding the 'one China' principle. This consensus consisted of four points:

1. Hungdah Chiu, "The Koo-Wang Talks and Intra-Chinese Relations," *American Journal of Chinese Studies* 2, no. 2 (October 1994): 226.
2. On the Connotation of "one China," approved by 8th Session of the National Unification Council, August 1, 1992.

- The two sides of the Taiwan Strait are agreed that there is only one China;

- Each side claims itself to be part of one China;

- Each acknowledges the existence of the other;

- Each is entitled to define one China differently from the other and state the definition orally.

After agreeing to set aside the Taiwan-China sovereignty issue, the chairmen of SEF and ARATS, Koo Chen-fu and Wang Dao-han, met in Singapore on April 27, 1993, and signed four agreements. These agreements related to how SEF and ARATS would conduct their affairs: notarizing certificates, registering mail service, convening regular meetings, and finally designating a time and place for future meetings. Both sides agreed to respect each other and to try to reach consensus. The Wang-Koo accord also listed the topics for future negotiations: smuggling and illegal immigration across the Taiwan Strait, fishery problems, airplane hijacking, protecting intellectual property rights, and others. This path-breaking agreement was achieved in the context of other public statements offered by both regimes.

The PRC regime continued to assert that it would not abandon the use of military force to facilitate reunification, because it feared that elements in Taiwan were advocating independence and it feared foreign interference, a veiled reference to U.S. sales of military weapons to Taiwan, a condition of the TRA. The ROC regime emphasized that it would not directly communicate with the PRC regime unless its leaders agreed to abandon the use of military force. Both regimes still defined the one-China principle very differently and offered different formulas by which China could be reunified. The gulf between the two regimes seemed cavernous, but the spirit of the April 29, 1993 Singapore meeting gave rise to what we refer to below as *one negotiating approach* that both regimes used to resolve the divided China problem. This détente was a momentous event in cross-Taiwan Strait relations since China's division in 1949.

But just as this negotiating approach began to take off, fueled by complex developments in both regimes during the 1980s, President Lee Teng-hui, a native Taiwanese, came up with his own ideas. Thus, despite the progress at the April 1993 Singapore meeting, by mid-June 1995 détente had collapsed, negotiations had ceased, and a major crisis in cross-Taiwan Strait relations had erupted.

Talks Begin and Then Are Aborted

The thaw in cross-strait relations during the 1980s and early 1990s had promoted an increment of trust between the two regimes. Beijing's leaders had opened up the mainland market to Taiwanese merchants and investors, encouraged people exchanges between the two sides, and discussed how to resolve airplane hijacking, smuggling, and fishing jurisdiction disputes. By these innovative actions, Beijing's leaders hoped to end China's civil war and resolve the Taiwan-Chinese sovereignty problem.

The PRC regime, through its Taiwan Affairs Office and the Information Office of the State Council, issued a White Paper of its own on August 31, 1993. This document informed the community of nation states of how China had divided and how the United States had perpetuated that division. It went on to say that only "one China" existed and that "Taiwan is an inalienable part of China, and the seat of China's central government is in Beijing."[3] In effect, just as the ROC regime had given the world

3. See Taiwan Affairs Office and Information Office State Council: *White Paper—the Taiwan Question and Reunification of China*, August 1993, Bejing, China..

its version of the one-China principle, so had the PRC regime presented to the world its interpretation of that principle.

Because both Chinese regimes still competed for international affirmations of their different claims of sovereignty of all China, Beijing and Taipei continued to view each other with mistrust.

Meanwhile, SEF and ARATS officials agreed to meet on August 29, 1993 in Beijing to discuss the issues of airplane hijacking, smuggling in the Taiwan Strait, and jurisdictional rights of fishing fleets. Further meetings were held on November 2, 1993, at Xiamen; on December 19, 1993, in Taipei; on March 25, 1994, in Beijing; on July 30, 1994, in Taipei; on December 22, 1994, in Nanjing; and finally on January 22, 1995, in Beijing. They paved the way for signing agreements on airplane hijacking and smuggling, with the fishing jurisdiction problem still to be decided.

In Beijing a convivial evening banquet on January 25 celebrated the two agreements reached for two of the three "functional issues."[4] But at midnight the SEF vice-chairman, Jiao Renhe, received a telephone call from Taiwan's MAC vice-chairman, Xiao Wanchang, informing him that SEF should sign either all three agreements or none of them (*lian huantao*). Jiao immediately faxed SEF chairman Koo Chen-fu in Taipei to resolve the new complication, but Koo never replied.

On January 26 an embarrassed Jiao told his ARATS counterpart it would not be possible to sign the two agreements without

4. Our account is based on interviews with Taiwan journalists who were in Beijing at the time and from the following Chinese sources: the Hong Kong *Da gong pao*, January 17, 1995, p. 1, which describes Jiao Renhe's sudden change of mind when he confided that he could not sign the two agreements. This scene occurred on the 10th floor of the Diaoyutai, where waiters already had posted a large banner celebrating the signing of the two agreements. See also *Zhongguo shibao*, January 27, 1995, p. 2, and *Gongshang ribao*, January 30, 1995, p. 2. Again, on January 29, 1995, a report appeared saying that both sides had convened for another six days of discussions to agree on the fishing jurisdiction issue but failed to do so because "they were constrained by the larger political issues involved"; see *Da gong bao*, January 29, 1995, p. 1.

signing an agreement on the fishing jurisdiction issue. ARATS's vice-chairman, Tang Shubei, replied, "Yesterday, we could sign for two agreements, but today the Taiwan side has changed its mind; only Taiwan can explain this." Jiao expressed his disappointment but added that he was only following instructions from MAC. Both sides met for another six days trying to hammer out an agreement on fishing jurisdiction but, having failed to do so, withdrew, having nothing to show for eighteen months of difficult negotiations.

Taiwan journalists opined that the talks had collapsed because MAC officials believed that it was better to adopt a tough negotiating stance than to give away too much. MAC officials also might have acted in accordance with President Lee's wishes. Lee, it was rumored, had conveyed to MAC chairman Xiao that a "linkage" strategy should be used for either extracting better terms from the Beijing side or for negotiating only for the sake of negotiating. The full, true story of why these important negotiations collapsed has yet to be told.

Whatever the true motives of the Taiwan leadership, this setback did not discourage Beijing. On January 30, President Jiang Zemin sent President Lee his eight-point policy for developing cross-strait relations within a "one China" and "one country, two systems" framework. Jiang's conciliatory proposal can be summarized as follows (see Appendix document 6).[5]

If both Chinese regimes believe there is only one China, Taiwan can have ties with other states but not on a government-to-government basis. Taiwan should not try to develop government-to-government relations, enter international organizations of nation-states, or try to create "two Chinas" or "one China, one Taiwan." Both sides should negotiate to resolve the divided China problem according to this one-China principle. The PRC regime wants to resolve this issue peacefully but will use

5. Winberg Chai, *Asian Affairs*, (summer 1999) pp. 100–101.

force if elements either within or outside Taiwan try to bring about an "independent Taiwan." Both sides should strive for peaceful unification because Chinese people should not fight Chinese people. As both sides negotiate, they might consider establishing three direct links to speed up their cooperation. By engaging each other in this way, both sides can also uphold and perpetuate the Chinese culture and way of life. The PRC always will respect the Taiwan people and their way of life; it wants Taiwan's leaders to visit the mainland. Hopefully, the people on both sides of the Taiwan Strait will arrange a meeting of national leaders.

The majority of Taiwan's people welcomed Jiang's conciliatory eight points, and the media endlessly discussed them. Although SEF and ARATS had not reached any agreements since the Singapore détente began, both agencies were always ready to negotiate. The respective chairmen of ARATS and SEF, Wang and Koo, were also scheduled for a second meeting in July 1995 in Hong Kong. While adhering to the Singapore détente negotiations, Beijing's authorities responded to the Lee administration's pragmatic foreign policy by contesting Taiwan's efforts to expand state-to-state relations with other nations. Then a series of events between 1994 and 1995 made the PRC regime abandon negotiations and adopt a hard-line strategy toward the ROC regime.

Lee's "Pragmatic Foreign Policy" and the Collapse of the Détente

The PRC regime continued to adhere to the Singapore détente even though the Lee administration began to implement a "pragmatic foreign policy" (*wushi waijiao*) as early as January 20, 1993, when the ROC Foreign Ministry published its first White Paper. This report explained how the ROC regime intended to conduct its foreign policy. It marked a radical change in foreign policy from that charted in the Chiang Kai-shek and Chiang Ching-kuo eras. The White Paper defined the new "pragmatic foreign policy" as a means to promote ROC regime relations with other nations "without any regard for the Mainland Factor."[6] The ROC regime would seek entry into international organizations and participate in their activities, return to the United Nations, and define the ROC regime as an "entity" of "one China."[7]

Taiwan had become increasingly isolated during the 1970s and 1980s, principally because of the strategies adopted by Chiang Kai-shek and Chiang Ching-kuo. Although relations between the regimes had steadily improved, President Lee seemed determined to reverse the decline of Taiwan's national sovereignty status. In 1989, at the GMD's 13th plenum, President Lee announced that the ROC regime would pursue a "pragmatic foreign policy" to "protect the sovereignty of our nation."[8]

By democratizing Taiwan and insisting that the PRC adopt the Taiwan model by democratizing and reforming its market economy, President Lee challenged the PRC leaders while he tried to implement his new pragmatic foreign policy to win international support for the ROC as a state independent of the PRC and outside the orbit of 'one China.' President Lee justified this new policy to his political supporters and critics at home by arguing that the people of Taiwan supported his new foreign policy, which many did.

As mentioned above, President Lee's negotiating team had disappointed Beijing's leaders in January 1995 by not signing two of the three agreements that SEF and ARATS had been negotiating for many months, insisting that all three problem issues first

6. Nanjing daxue Taiwan wenti yanjiusuo, comp., *Haixia liangan guanxi jizhi,1949–1998* (A chronology of cross-Taiwan Strait relations, 1949–1998) (Beijing: Jiuzhou tushu chubanshe, 1999), p. 494.

7. Ibid.

8. Wu Xinxing, *Zhenghe lilun yu liangan guanxi zhi yanjiu* (Studies of general theory and cross-strait relations) (Taipei: Wunan tushu chubanshe, 1999), p.213.

be agreed on. Moreover, Lee had not responded to Jiang Zemin's, January 30, 1995, conciliatory eight-point proposal to the Lee administration. Then on March 8, 1995, Beijing's leaders suddenly learned that Taiwan's powerful lobby in Washington, D.C., had helped persuade the U.S. Congress to pass a concurrent resolution, by a vote of 97 to 1 in the Senate and 396 to 0 in the House, granting a visa for an unprecedented visit by Lee Teng-hui to the United States.[9] At the same time, Taiwan was lobbying for membership in the United Nations.

Furious at President Lee's repeated efforts to win foreign, especially U.S. government recognition of Taiwan as an independent, democratic, sovereign state, Beijing's leaders, without any warning, ordered their military forces to fire live ammunition in a sea-and-air maneuver off the coastal areas opposite Taiwan on March 12, 1995. The next day a unit fired guided missiles into the waters off Taiwan's Kaohsiung harbor.[10] These war games, the most audacious ever conducted near Taiwan by the PRC regime, shocked Taiwan, angered the Lee administration, and deeply disturbed Washington.

Despite Beijing's hard-line approach, President Lee decided on April 8, 1995, to answer the eight points proposed by President Jiang Zemin with a six-point reply.[11] President Lee began by asserting that the PRC regime must "respect" the fact that Taiwan and mainland China have been governed by "two sovereign political entities" since 1949 and that a display of respect was a necessary condition for negotiating China's unification. He then alluded to all Chinese people having pride in Chinese culture and the importance of promoting goodwill and bilateral exchange. He urged that bilateral trade and communications be expanded and offered Taiwan's help to improve mainland China's agriculture,

9. Winberg Chai, *Asian Affairs* (summer 1999), p. 74.
10. Ibid.
11. Ibid., pp. 101–2.

economy, and living standards. He then insisted that both regimes participate in international organizations, meaning that both regimes' leaders might meet at annual Asia-Pacific Economic Cooperation meetings. But the PRC must give up the use of force and set aside its argument that force is required to stop "foreign interference and Taiwan independence." Finally, only if both regimes cooperated could democracy and prosperity be ensured for Hong Kong and Macao. In effect, President Lee merely repeated the conditions previously demanded by Taipei of Beijing; the only new offer was Taiwan sharing its agriculture development experience with the mainland regime. Lee's reply was likely regarded as an insult by Beijing's authorities.[12]

Even so, on May 27–28, 1995, the SEF and ARATS discussion teams met in Beijing and agreed to hold a second round of Wang-Koo talks. Beijing's leaders, hoping that this meeting might revitalize the Singapore détente, still did not believe that President Lee would travel to the United States in June to speak at Cornell University, his alma mater. Beijing's decision to continue the Singapore détente talks reflected that leadership's hope that negotiations under the one-China principle could be continued (even though the two sides adhered to different interpretations of that principle). As for Taipei's leaders, they hoped that, by continuing the Singapore détente negotiations, Beijing might ultimately agree to their conditions (as set forth in Taipei's two White Papers). Meanwhile, the Lee administration was perfectly content to promote its pragmatic foreign policy.

Beijing's leaders were shocked when, on June 9, 1995, President Lee spoke at Cornell. His speech, titled "The People's Aspirations Are Always in My Heart," described Taiwan's economic and political miracles and declared that those experiences could be adopted by the PRC regime, paving the way for the unification

12. Impressions gleaned from interviews with Taiwan experts in Beijing.

of China. The president emphasized that "ever since I have assumed office, I have always relied on the people's needs and hopes as my political beacon light." Expressing hope that the PRC regime would draw lessons from Taiwan's experiences and his style of governance, the president stated that Beijing must abandon the use of force so that there could be a "win-win" strategy for both sides, to "protect the interests of the Chinese people and enable mutual respect to lead toward China's unification under a system of developing freedom and equality for both the rich and the poor."[13]

Lee's speech further angered Beijing's leaders, who by now identified Lee as a separatist and a traitor. The events of summer and fall 1995, followed by more military exercises and missile launches in spring 1996, need not be repeated here. The display of PRC military force, which brought two U.S. aircraft carriers to Taiwan waters, produced much speculation and mixed reactions within the United States, Taiwan, and the greater Asia-Pacific region. Many analysts and power holders now realized that the Taiwan problem was serious, that the PRC regime meant business, and that the ROC regime should not anger the Beijing leadership. Others argued that the United States should adopt a tougher stand toward this emerging power by containing the PRC. Still others, particularly in Taiwan, believed that the PRC government would not risk war over Taiwan and that if its leaders did take such action, the U.S. government would militarily intervene to protect Taiwan.

The PRC leadership had tried to clarify the ground rules for how the divided China problem should be resolved. It wanted the Singapore détente negotiations revitalized and focused on resolv-

13. Zhang Zenghe, *Liangan guanxi bianjianshi*, p. 370; President Lee's speech in Chinese is cited in Wu Xinxing, *Zhenghe lilun yu liangan guanxi zhi yanjiu as Min chi soyu, hang-zai wo-xin* (The people's aspirations are always in my heart), pp. 513–21.

ing the Taiwan-China sovereignty issue using Beijing's federation model of "one country, two systems." But if Taiwan declared independence, it would use force to resolve the divided China problem. Meanwhile, the United States should uphold the one-China principle and not intervene in the affairs of the Chinese people, especially by selling weapons to Taiwan. As for U.S. weapon sales to Taiwan, Beijing's leaders hoped that the U.S. would comply with point six of the U.S.-PRC Joint Communiqué of August 17, 1982 (see Appendix, document 4), which stipulated the phasing out of all weapon sales to Taiwan. At the same time, the PRC regime intended to block the Lee administration's "pragmatic foreign policy."

On May 20, 1996, President Lee was inaugurated as the first popularly elected president in Chinese history. In his acceptance speech, he praised Taiwan's democracy and its people and emphasized that the country was entering a new era and therefore must deepen democracy; he also called for improving economic development, reforming society's judicial, educational, and cultural systems, and managing "a great Taiwan [and] nurturing a new Chinese culture." To achieve these goals, the president intended to invite political leaders and other representatives to give their views about "future national development" and thus build a consensus to "launch the country into a new era."[14] Toward the end of his speech, President Lee blamed the PRC for not recognizing the existence of the ROC and for orchestrating a campaign to damage his reputation. He also scolded Beijing's leaders for conducting war games, but promised dialogue with them and rejected the course of "Taiwan independence." He stated his willingness to "meet with the top leadership of the Chinese Communists Party for a direct exchange of views in order to

14. See "Inaugural Address: Lee Teng-hui, President, Republic of China, May 20, 1996.

open up a new era of communication and cooperation between the two sides." By brushing aside the recent crisis, President Lee was launching a peace offensive of his own.

But had he promised anything really different from what he had done in the past? Developments from mid-1996 to early 2000 show that he had not.

Beijing's leaders now responded positively to Lee's speech. At a June 26, 1996 press conference, Jiang Zemin said that negotiations for peaceful reunification could begin under the one-China principle. But neither side was able to persuade the other to return to the Singapore détente negotiations.

For example, in August 1996 at a high-level meeting in the office of the president, President Lee stated that "the ROC's policy must be rooted in Taiwan, and, in order to take off, there must be a sense of 'no haste, be patient' (*jieji yongren*) so that 'the ROC can gradually, unswervingly achieve China's unification.'"[15] At a September 14, 1996, National Management Conference, President Lee introduced this new policy of "avoiding haste by being patient," meaning that the ROC government would monitor business investments and prohibit those exceeding US $50 million. Therefore, when the Taiwanese tycoon Wang Yongqing went to Xiamen in the fall of 1996 to discuss building a large electrical power station, the ROC government asked him to withdraw. Although high-profile Taiwan businesspersons criticized the government's new policy, the Lee administration did not yield. Lee's goal was to slow down Taiwan-mainland China trade and investment to prevent ROC dependency on the PRC economy.

At the same time, the ROC regime increased its purchases of defensive weapons from France and the United States. As the U.S. and Japanese governments began reappraising their security

15. Chen Zujian, *Maishang liangan tampan* (Toward détente between mainland China and Taiwan) (Hong Kong: Taipingyang shiji chubanshe, 1998), p. 411.

treaty to consider whether to defend Taiwan under special circumstances, discussions also focused on the desirability of including Taiwan in a new theater missile defense system.

The PRC continued to call on the ROC to resume negotiations based on the one-China principle, but the ROC insisted on discussing only "functional" issues. In early 1998 ARATS chairman Wang Daohan met with a delegation of private individuals from Taiwan and informed them that the PRC was prepared to talk with Taiwan's representatives about how the sovereignty of Taiwan-China might be negotiated under the principle of one China. Then in April 1999 Wang Daohan offered a new China principle that both regimes could embrace in order to return to the negotiating table.

> There is only "one" China in the world and Taiwan is a part of China. At this time, there is no reunified China. Both sides ought to cooperate with all their effort, under the "one China" principle, to negotiate on an equal basis and reach a consensus on the reunification of China. The sovereignty and territory of a nation-state cannot be divided. Taiwan's political status still ought to be discussed under the premise of "one China."[16]

According to Wang, both sides should negotiate as equal partners under the principle of one China. To be sure, the PRC regime had always preferred its federalist formula of "one country, two systems," as spelled out in its White Paper, assigning Taiwan to be the region and the PRC to be the "political center" of "one China." But Wang's proposal opened the door to the possibility that because the "sovereignty and territory of a nation-state cannot be divided," the sovereignty of Taiwan-China could be equally

16. See Wang Daohan, "Liangan heping di zwei xinjiyu" (The most recent favorable opportunity for peace across the Taiwan Strait), *Yazhou Zhoukan* (Asian weekly) April 19–25, 1999, pp. 18–19.

shared between the two regimes, perhaps under a commonwealth or economic union arrangement.

Because the PRC regime had repeatedly expressed its White Paper's interpretation of the one country, two system formula, the ROC regime had no difficulty persuading many people, especially in Taiwan, that Beijing did not respect Taiwan as an equal and, therefore, that entering negotiations with the PRC placed Taiwan at a great security risk as well as at a distinct disadvantage.

To counter the PRC regime's one country, two system formula, the ROC insisted that it had every right to try to expand its international space and to wait until the PRC agreed to its unification guidelines formula before accepting negotiations with the mainland China authorities. These arguments appealed to Taiwan's people, who were increasingly telling public opinion pollsters that they considered themselves Taiwanese but not Chinese.[17] The Taiwan authorities, therefore, continued their "pragmatic foreign policy," refused to negotiate with the PRC until conditions set forth in their unification guidelines were met, and stoked the fires of Taiwanese nationalism. The Lee administration made no effort to return to the Singapore détente negotiations; when Wang formulated the new one-China principle, which left open negotiation of the divided China sovereignty issue, the ROC regime was not listening.

After both sides had repeatedly called for direct negotiations according to conditions unacceptable to both, the deputy secre-

---

17. By 1998 the MAC polls showed the share of people identifying themselves as only Taiwanese as 38 percent compared to nearly 17 percent in September 1992 and January 1993. The share identifying themselves as only Chinese had fallen to 12 percent compared to 46 percent in 1992–93. Meanwhile, those regarding themselves as being both Taiwanese and Chinese was around half in October 1998 compared to around one-third in 1992–93. Thus a subtle shift in the pattern of cultural identity has taken place in the 1990s. See the Mainland Affairs Council, Executive Yuan, "Public Opinion on Cross-Strait Relations in the Republic of China," November 1998.

tary-generals of the SEF and ARATS met in February 1998 and agreed to facilitate SEF chairman Koo Chen-fu's visit to the PRC. On October 19, 1998, Koo and his delegation returned from Beijing after having spent six days visiting Wang Daohan in Shanghai and paid their respects to President Jiang Zemin in Beijing. Both sides agreed that Wang would reciprocate the Koo visit by leading a delegation to Taiwan in 1999, at a time to be worked out by SEF and ARATS. Both sides seemed poised to resume their negotiations despite high levels of distrust. But this partial détente was short-lived.

Lee's "State-to-State Relationship" Concept and the Cross-Strait Relations Impasse

President Lee's feelings toward Taiwan and its relationship with China had surfaced when a Japanese journalist interviewed the president in May 1994. Speaking in Japanese, President Lee was quoted as saying that the GMD was an "outside force" when it came to Taiwan in 1945. For that reason, explained the president, "we must make the GMD into a party for the Taiwanese people." He went on to say that he had "endured all kinds of conditions until now, because I carry the feelings of the people in my heart. The Taiwanese people expect me to act, and I am now trying to take action." Finally, the president compared himself to Moses, saying that "when we think about the Taiwanese people and their sacrifices regarding the February 28, 1947, incident, I can only conclude that my role is like that in the exodus from Egypt."[18] Taken together, President Lee's interview gave the impression that he had no "true feelings of being Chinese" and that the Taiwanese were not like the Chinese.

On July 9, 1999, when President Lee Teng-hui was inter-

---

18. Chao and Myers, *The First Chinese Democracy*, p. 292.

viewed by the Deutsche Welle Broadcasting Company in Germany, he stated that constitutional reform in Taiwan had placed cross-strait relations on "a state-to-state relationship or at least a special state-to-state relationship, rather than an internal relationship between a legitimate government and a renegade group, or between a central government and a local government."[19] President Lee's comment angered Beijing and set off a firestorm of discussion and debate. The day after Lee's statement, Koo Chen-fu, SEF chairman, reaffirmed that the cross-strait negotiations were "state-to-state talks." Beijing's leaders denounced President Lee as denying the "one China" principle, splitting Taiwan from China, and immediately canceled Wang Daohan's trip to Taipei. Beijing's leaders feared that President Lee might insert his new two-state theory (*liangguo lun*) into the ROC constitution, an act they said would mean declaring Taiwan's independence.

Having consolidated his power by late 1996, President Lee was gradually deviating from the GMD's "one China" policy. He had labeled the GMD as an "outside force," and then redefined the ROC as the "ROC on Taiwan." Finally, he conceptualized China as already divided into two sovereign countries, and their relations as "state-to-state." According to President Lee, the struggle between the two sides had shifted from a struggle to legitimize different "one China" principles to a struggle of one Taiwan versus one China, or two separate Chinese states.

The "state-to-state" concept was not an impromptu address by President Lee. It had been thoroughly prepared for some time. Taiwan's media disclosed that Ying Chong-wen, the Chief of the National Security Bureau, had suggested to President Lee that he establish, in August 1998, a Caucus for Strengthening ROC Sovereign Nation Status. Within a year, the Caucus submitted a

19. Mainland Affairs Council, *Taipei Speaks Up: Special State-to-State-Relationship: Republic of China's Policy Documents* (Taipei: Mainland Affairs Council, Executive Yuan, Republic of China, 1999), pp. 1–2.

report, which Lee immediately approved. The report indicated that since the revision of the constitution in 1991, and after, the sovereignty and administrative authority of ROC has been confined to Taiwan; thus the relations between Taiwan and mainland should be defined as "state-to-state." The report recommended revising the constitution and related laws, approving new laws by referendums, and gradually abrogating the National Unification Guidelines (NUG). As a first step, Taiwan would not use such terms as "one China," "one China means ROC," "a divided China," and "one China with respective interpretations." In brief, Taiwan was to become an independent, sovereign nation that had seceded from China.[20]

Why had Lee waited until July 1999 to declare that Taiwan must assume a state-to-state relationship with mainland China without conceding that both regimes were still part of China—the government's official line in the past? The explanation PRC officials and scholars offer is that he feared ever-increasing interactions between the two sides would increase Taiwan's economic dependency on mainland China. After negotiations began between SEF and ARATS, cross-strait people-to-people and business exchanges had thrived. Bilateral trade and economic cooperation were complementary and increasingly beneficial to both sides. In 1999, Taiwan's investment in the mainland accounted for more than 40 US$ billion, and Taiwan's trade surplus with the mainland was nearly 90 US$ billion.[21] Lee's "avoiding haste by being patient" policy had not slowed this process. More importantly, Wang Daohan was scheduled to visit Taiwan in the fall of that year to revive cross-strait talks. Lee, determined to move out of China's orbit and to pursue Taiwan independence, perhaps

20. "The Demise of Restoration of the Two-State Theory?" *United Daily News*, July 9, 2001, p. A3.

21. Xinhua Agency's Commentator, "Maintaining 'Two-State Theory'—A Betrayal to Taiwanese People," *Renmin Ribao*, July 30, 1999.

worried that Wang's visit would lead to a warming of cross-strait relations and inspire a new wave of "mainland fever" on the island.

Was President Lee trying to influence a new debate in the United States after Sino-American relations had soured because NATO, in the spring of 1998, had bombed the Chinese embassy in Belgrade? Lee's new concept of Taiwan's status certainly irritated Beijing and aggravated Sino-US relations. Yet Lee seemed not to have cared, probably because he was now a lame duck president. To Lee's disappointment, however, President Clinton had telephoned President Jiang Zemin on July 18, 1999, reiterating that the US firmly upholds the "one China" principle, and that there is no change in US policy toward Taiwan.[22] Major US media and leading China experts criticized Lee's statement, and some even labeled him as a "trouble maker." In early September 1999, a high-ranking official of the US State Department told a visiting official from Taiwan's Presidential Office in Washington that Taiwan should not surprise the US when it makes a policy statement. The Taiwan representative replied that there was no change in Taiwan's policy toward the mainland, and that Taiwan would neither revise the Constitution and related laws nor abrogate the NUC.

22. *Renmin Ribao*, July 19, 1999.

4. The Challenge of Taiwan Independence

Taiwan's politics are not ethnic in nature as some Taiwan experts assert.[1] "Taiwanese sentiment" did not become mainstream until the late 1980s and 1990s when a certain group of politicians began to champion Taiwan independence and the mainland China authorities threatened Taiwan with the use of force. Now the beliefs that foreshadowed Taiwan nationalism have become a new force in Taiwan's political life and have weakened GMD power. Consider this matter in the historical perspective of the last 350 years.

First settled by aboriginal tribes and then by Chinese immigrants, Taiwan came under Qing state control when Admiral Shih Lang landed on the island in October 1683, after defeating the forces of the Ming under the leadership of Zheng Chenggong. The Qing quickly incorporated Taiwan as a prefecture of Fujian province, just across the Taiwan Strait. Waves of Chinese immigrants began colonizing the western side of the island, farming the land to produce tea, sugar, and rice for export to the mainland. When the official Yu Yong traveled to Taiwan in 1697, he raved about China's influence over the island. "The prestige of our dynasty [the Qing] extends far and wide. The rebel Zheng [Koxinga] has expressed his allegiance. Taiwan lies far beyond the Eastern

1. See John Thacik, "Taiwan's Majority Won't Stand for Unification with China," *China Brief*, Heritage Foundation, Washington, DC, Volume 1, Issue 3, August 7, 2001.

Ocean; from antiquity until today, there has never been a tribute mission sent to China." Now we have divided the land "into districts and counties, established governmental offices, levied taxes and tribute, opened sea routes for continuous traffic back and forth, and added a ninth to the eight prefecture of Fujian; it is truly a great feat."[2]

By the mid-eighteenth century the Qing had Sinicized a large portion of the island's occupants and was even transforming the culture and society of the aboriginal tribes. After 1885, the Qing court conferred provincial status on the island and began strengthening its defenses and infrastructure. As a province of imperial China, its scholars, administrators, ordinary people, and many Aborigines, saw themselves as Chinese. There was no integrated native Taiwanese sentiment or "Taiwan independent movement."

The first Sino-Japanese War ended in China's defeat, and forced the Qing government, on April 17, 1895, to cede the islands of Taiwan and the Pescadores to Japan. Even fifty years later the overwhelming majority of Taiwanese still regarded themselves as Chinese and only a minority identified themselves as Japanese. "The national sentiment of being Taiwanese," described in a Japanese Governor's Office's reference book published in 1939, "stemmed from their identity of being a Chinese (Han) nation and having a 5,000-year cultural heritage. . . . The sentiment of Taiwanese regarding China as their motherland is an undeniable fact . . ."[3]

But under Japanese colonial rule, a minority of Taiwan's

2. Emma Jinhua Jeng, *Taiwan's Imagined Geography: Chinese Colonial Travel Writing and Pictures, 1683–1895* (Cambridge: Harvard University Asia Leva, 2004), p. 262.

3. Police Department, Governor's Office of Taiwan, *Police History of Governor's Office of Taiwan, Volume 11, Security Situation since Occupation—A History of Social Movement*, July 1939, pp. 1–2.

native elite received Japanese imperial education and greatly admired Japan's modernity and administration of Taiwan. Such elite sentiments would have an important impact on Taiwan's future political landscape. Even so, many Taiwanese resisted the Japanese occupation, especially when Japan invaded China in 1937.

The desire for Taiwanese independence should have diminished after Taiwan reverted to Nationalist China's control on October 25, 1945, but that did not occur. Many Taiwanese suffered under unruly nationalist troops; the gap in living standards and life styles grew between Taiwanese and mainlanders; mainlanders took most of the Taiwan Provincial administrative jobs and Japanese physical assets; and poor language communication fomented anger and a desire for revenge among the Taiwanese.

These cultural and economic disparities diminished Taiwanese expectations and triggered a large urban uprising in the first two weeks of March 1947. The uprising had begun on the evening of February 28th and ended around mid March when nationalist troops brutally abolished the urban councils set up by the Taiwanese to keep order and negotiate a political settlement with the Taiwan Provincial Governor Chen Yi.

Subsequent Taiwan Provincial Government authorities, followed by Chiang Kai-shek administration officials in 1949, covered up the uprising and its harsh suppression and deluded themselves into believing that communists and their supporters had caused the tragedy. By refusing to tell the truth and promote a healing process to win over the Taiwanese to its cause, the new regime never placated those Taiwanese elites and their families scarred by the violence of the February 1947 uprising. That generation of Taiwanese never forgot the early years of Nationalist Government rule, and many, like the young Lee Teng-hui, yearned for a Republic of Taiwan free of China's influence.

Some Taiwanese elites like Guo Guoti and Li Wanju partici-

pated in the political system established by the GMD, coura-
geously criticized its officials, and advocated reforms. Other
Taiwanese elites like Huang Chaoqin concealed their true feelings
and served as Chairmen of the Taiwan Provincial Assembly from
1946 until 1963.[4]

After 1950, ethnically classified population data revealed that
98.3 percent of Taiwan's population were Chinese (Han), and
descendants of immigrants from Fujian and Guangdong provinces, while 1.7 percent were Taiwan aboriginals.[5] Among the former, more than 80 percent came from southern Fujian, and spoke
the Hok-Lo dialect. Another 15 percent were Hakka, mostly from
Guangdong. These two linguistic groups competed in local politics until 1949, when the GMD-led government moved to the
island and enforced Mandarin as the official language.

By 1950, nearly two million mainlanders had arrived on the
island. These new immigrants, mostly former government officials, soldiers, teachers, and small businessmen, were referred to
as "*waisheng ren* (mainlanders)." "Those who arrived before 1950
were regarded as "*bensheng ren* (Taiwan natives)." According to
1992 statistics, "*waisheng ren*" and their second and third generations comprised 13 percent of the Taiwan population.[6]

The "*bensheng ren*" and "*waisheng ren*" division did not constitute a source of conflict in Taiwan's politics unless instigated
by powerful, influential local elites. In the first decades of GMD
rule, the major central government positions were held by elites
from provinces of China. The local governments below the township level were dominated by Taiwanese elites. By the early
1960s, when hopes for recovering the mainland were fading and

4. Steven E. Phillips, *Between Assimilation and Independence: The Taiwanese Encounter Nationalist China, 1945–1950* (Stanford, California: Stanford
University Press, 2003), p. 136.

5. Ibid., p. 6.

6. See *China Times*, November 28, 1992.

the ethnic composition within the central government seemed likely to continue, more Taiwanese began seeking power in the central governance and the GMD welcomed them.

The Dangwai Movement

Taiwan native candidates increased their seats in central and local legislatures during the first supplementary elections that began in late 1969 and 1972. The ROC regime introduced these new elections to deepen Taiwan's democratization. At the same time, non-GMD politicians *(dangwai)* were competing in growing numbers in local elections in late 1978, in what can be called the beginning of real democracy or a fair electoral process. Subsequently, in late 1978 *dangwai* candidates won 19 percent of the additional National Assembly seats and 17 percent of the additional Legislative Yuan seats in the newly established supplementary national representative elections.[7] This election breakthrough from the *dangwai* signaled the advance of Taiwan's democracy.

These *"dangwai"* politicians were born in Taiwan of parents who strongly identified with the island's culture and language and had lived for one or more generations in Taiwan. Although critical of the GMD's unfair behavior toward the Taiwanese, the *dangwai* did not support Taiwan's independence movement, but wanted political power. The majority regarded themselves as Chinese and advocated that Taiwan be unified with China.[8] This emerging political opposition toward the GMD was a mixture of different political factions trying to win elections to achieve diverse political goals.

In the 1970s and 1980s the *dangwai* expanded its influence

7. Linda Chao and Ramon Myers, *The First Chinese Democracy* (Baltimore: Johns Hopkins University Press, 1998), pp. 64–65.
8. Ibid., p. 74.

as the GMD was trying to recruit more Taiwanese. These new *dangwai*, unlike their predecessors of the 1950s and 1960s, increasingly resorted to street demonstrations to test the government's resolve. Many overseas Taiwanese in the U.S. and Japan were advocating a Taiwan nation-state and Taiwan independence.[9] More opponents of the GMD regime became active in local politics, and they learned how to win voter support. As the GMD regime relaxed control and the opposition pressed for establishing a political party, street violence occurred as it had in December 1979. In Kaohsiung City, the largest clash took place between native Taiwanese and GMD authorities since February 28, 1947. For the first time some "*dangwai*" opponents explained this violent event as a struggle between native Taiwanese and "outside" GMD rulers, and some people began speaking out for a "Taiwan nation."

The Nationalist Government still imposed martial law, and those radical Taiwanese who favored a Taiwanese independent movement sought refuge abroad, fleeing first to Hong Kong and then to Japan or the U.S.[10] As time passed, more political dissidents even went abroad to join the anti GMD regime movement.

An Opposition Political Party Forms

In September 1986, a new political party, calling itself the Democratic Progressive Party (DPP), illegally formed. The GMD's chairman, Chiang Ching-kuo, did not take any action to suppress this new party. DPP leaders did not advocate the creation of an independent Taiwan state in the party charter, but they did demand that the party would "allow Taiwan's people to determine

9. See Yin Zhangyi, p. 9.
10. Yin Zhangyi (Professor of History, Furen University, Taiwan), "The Formation and Development of Taiwan Sentiment—A Historical Perspective," *Taiwan Studies*, Beijing, No. 2 1994, pp. 24–25.

the future of Taiwan and develop diplomatic ties with other nations . . . ." Thus, the DPP stopped short of calling for Taiwan to separate from mainland China and establish a Republic of Taiwan having a new constitution, flag, and anthem.[11]

The political opposition continued to campaign on the platform of building democracy by constitutional reform and expanding direct elections. But in 1989, some DPP leaders, for the first time, declared their support for a higher goal than Taiwan's democratization: to establish a Republic of Taiwan with a new constitution affirming Taiwan's separation from mainland China. At the DPP's 5th plenum in October 1991, party members inserted the following into the DPP charter: "The residents of Taiwan will decide their destiny, and the Taiwan people will vote on whether to establish a Republic of Taiwan and redraft the constitution." Party delegates also agreed to campaign publicly for Taiwan independence to win voter support.[12] The DPP and its supporters, whose families had lived in a Taiwan separated from the mainland's governance since 1895 (except between late 1945 and 1949), now believed that creating a Republic of Taiwan independent of the mainland was Taiwan's destiny.

The GMD government had always relied on its education system to strengthen Chinese culture and Chinese identity as well as promote Mandarin as the national language. Yet separatist sentiments and a Taiwan independence movement still slowly emerged. Why was that possible? We refer to some causal factors.

First, many Taiwanese bitterly resented Nationalist Government corruption and the abuse of its power and harsh suppression of dissidents. Taiwan's one-party system had lasted far longer than many believed justified. A deep hatred of GMD by the few had included enmity toward China and disgust with Chi-

---

11. Linda Chao and Ramon Myers, p. 134.
12. Ibid., p. 278.

nese culture. As democracy deepened in Taiwan, more people felt free to criticize the government. When the state authorities over-reacted toward Taiwanese criticisms, those actions fueled more criticism of the GMD-led regime.

Second, the two sides of the strait had been separated since 1949. It was not until October 1987, nearly 40 years later, that Taiwan's authorities permitted its residents to visit the mainland. But considerable misunderstanding and estrangement had arisen between these two societies. Four decades of anti-communism education by the GMD authorities had made people suspicious of the mainland regime and its people. Taiwan residents had acquired an anti-communist-phobia, and they saw China as back-ward and more corrupt than Taiwan.

Third, Beijing's claim that it solely represented China also motivated some Taiwanese to justify their building an independ-ent nation-state. Some public surveys showed that when the mainland authorities took a harsh stance toward Taiwan, for example, threatening the use of force, the percentage of those polled who identified themselves as Chinese or both Chinese and Taiwanese declined while the percentage of those who identified with being Taiwanese rose. Table 1 below shows that after 1996, when the mainland China authorities launched missiles into the waters off the Taiwan coast in response to President Lee's trip to America in June 1995, a new trend of thinking began to evolve in Taiwan; more people began seeing themselves as Taiwanese rather than Chinese.

To be sure, a growing sense of being Taiwanese and not Chi-nese, along with a dream of an independent Taiwan, had emerged after October 1945, but only by the early 1990s did a mainstream public awareness of being Taiwanese begin to grow stronger. A public poll conducted among college students in 1987 had revealed that only 8.8 percent identified themselves as Taiwanese; 14.9 percent for both Taiwanese and Chinese; 49.7 percent—both

Table 1. Public Polling of Self-Identity Change
Among Taiwan Residents (1991–2001)

Month and Year	Taiwanese (%)	Taiwanese and Chinese (%)	Chinese (%)	Number of Respondents
December 1991	19.8	54.8	25.5	926
June 1992	19.5	50.9	29.6	2774
July 1994	21.7	49.9	28.4	1115
November 1995	31.0	49.1	19.9	1100
June 1996	27.1	57.5	15.5	1086
May 1997	33.5	46.2	20.3	1172
February 1998	35.3	48.2	16.6	1165
November 1999	36.2	53.0	10.8	1903
March 2000	35.1	53.0	11.9	1219
June 2001	38.9	50.5	10.7	1018

Source: These data were obtained from polls conducted by the Election Studies Center of National Chengchi University

Chinese and Taiwanese; 35.5 percent—Chinese; 5.9 percent—other.[13] By November 1999 it is clear from Table 1 that a decisive shift in ethnic identity had occurred after 1991.

As Beijing's leaders promoted economic reform in the 1980s, Taiwan's authorities permitted more of its citizens to visit the mainland. Cross-strait trade and social exchanges greatly increased. The mainland appeared more appealing for more Taiwanese. The old Communism-phobia slowly evaporated. But why did the sentiment for Taiwan independence not wane? Some politicians, like President Lee Teng-hui, successfully instilled in the peoples' mind a contempt for China and its inward directed civilization. Lee also referred to a collective Taiwanese memory of sorrow and frustration, and at the same time his leadership actions provoked China to behave as a bully toward Taiwan, thus angering more Taiwanese and making them, like Lee, contemptuous and resentful of mainland China.

13. See Yin Zhangyi, p. 13.

During his twelve-year (1988–2000) tenure as GMD chairman and Taiwan's president, Lee encouraged the people to "return to their native roots" (or to make "Taiwan first"). At the same time, he subtly encouraged more GMD members to take pride in being "new Taiwanese" and reject China's bullying. As early as 1994, Lee had labeled the GMD of the late forties as an "alien regime." And so, just as détente was being achieved between these two Chinese regimes in the early 1990s, a generational political power shift was also taking place in Taiwan. Many GMD elders retired.

Taiwan's polity had rapidly democratized, and more Taiwanese believed they should celebrate their Taiwanese identity. More people rejected the idea that Taiwan should have a special relationship with mainland China's regime, and insisted that Taiwan be treated as a normal state. A majority in the DPP believed this way.

Meanwhile, President Lee, in August 1997, ordered the Ministry of Education and the National Institute of Compilation and Translation to introduce three new textbooks emphasizing Taiwan history, society, and geography; these materials dramatically devalued the "identification of Taiwan as part of China."[14]

Even so, around two-thirds of the population still preferred to maintain cross-strait relations in their current state. They wanted both sides to negotiate agreements to improve mutual trust and expand economic and social exchanges. They even welcomed President Lee's pragmatic foreign policy as long as it did not anger Beijing's leaders.[15]

14. Christopher Hughes and Robert Stone, "Nation-Building and Curriculum Reform in Hong Kong and Taiwan," *China Quarterly*, no. 160 (December 1999): 985–86.

15. In the MAC opinion polls for issues such as the pace of cross-strait relations, views on pragmatic foreign policy, and so on, the responses are not categorized according to groups favoring the status quo, independence, and so forth.

President Lee had rallied considerable public opinion behind him when he campaigned for the Taiwan presidency in the spring of 1996. His rhetoric tapped into Taiwanese sentiments about heritage and democracy. Lee repeatedly told the people he was justified in delaying political negotiations with Beijing's leaders because Taiwan's democracy depended on its sovereignty being determined by the wishes of the people (*zhuchuan zaimin*) and not by Beijing's bullying. At the same time, President Lee repeatedly imposed unrealistic conditions on Beijing's leaders by demanding they rapidly democratize and develop a capitalist market economy before the ROC regime would begin political negotiations. Further, President Lee always reminded Beijing that Taiwan was already a sovereign country, and he avoided mentioning the one-China principle as a pre-condition for entering into negotiations.

By lauding the virtues of the ROC regime's democracy and its capitalist market economy, President Lee projected the mainland China regime as a communist dictatorship bullying a little democracy. By standing up to Beijing's leaders, Lee won the hearts and minds of many citizens, especially in the spring 1996 presidential elections. Then, in December 1998, he coined the phrase "new Taiwanese" and praised Taiwan's current multiethnic identity, implying that Taiwan was no longer a Chinese society. In these ways, the Lee administration redefined Taiwan's relationship with mainland China while avoiding political negotiations to resolve the divided China issue by means of long term reunification.

In late February and early March of 2000, the most fiercely fought election in Taiwan's history took place since local elections began in 1950. Five slates of presidential and vice presidential candidates competed; three ran so closely that it was impossible to predict the outcome even on election day, Saturday, March 18. After 83 percent of all eligible voters cast their ballots between 8: 00 a.m. and 4:00 p.m. The DPP candidate, Chen Shui-bian, and his running mate, Annette Lu, triumphed, winning 39.9 percent of the votes, followed by independent James Soong with 36.8 percent, and the GMD candidate, Lien Chan, obtaining only 23.1 percent. This election, closely watched around the world, was the most important event in Taiwan's political history. The GMD party, which had controlled Taiwan's government for fifty-five years, had lost its power to govern. Many analysts in Taiwan asserted that Lee, in devious ways, had helped the DPP to win the election.

Several years later, Lee explained why he had promoted a "Taiwanese sentiment" which had helped the DPP to win power. In a speech addressed to his "friends," he said the following: "During 50 years of Japanese rule, although Japan was unsuccessful in its 'Japanization' of Taiwan, its greatest contribution was to promote in elite thinking the nation-state idea. Japan also created modern administrative, judicial and financial institutions, and put Taiwan on the evolutionary course to become a modern nation. . . . Therefore, without any sentiment of being Taiwanese, without loving Taiwan, Taiwan's future will be in jeopardy."[16] Lee then said:

"I was asked why I, the chairman of the GMD, should have deceived the party?" Lee candidly said: "Because I have always strived to transfer power from the 'outside regime'—the GMD—to the 'real' Taiwanese. If you do not know that, you are stupid!"[17]

The DPP Devalues Taiwan as a Chinese Society

In his inaugural address on May 15, 2000, President Chen Shui-bian pledged that his government would not declare Taiwan inde-

16. Speech on the founding meeting of the Association of Friends of Lee Teng-hui in Keelong, *World Journal*, October 13, 2002, p. A5.
17. Ibid.

pendence. He made no mention that his party would try to remove all vestiges of Chinese symbols and ideas while strengthening the belief system that Taiwan's people were Taiwanese and not Chinese.

Speaking to the congress of the pro-Taiwan independence organization—FAPA—on January 13, 2002, President Chen announced that he approved adding "Taiwan" on the cover of the country's passport right after the nation's name "ROC." He made clear that this was the "best gift" for the 20th anniversary of FAPA. Soon after, the Ministry of Foreign Affairs announced that it intended to rename its non-official offices in foreign countries as "Taiwan Representative Offices." In the meantime, the Government Information Office replaced the term ROC—the country's name used since the founding of the ROC—with "Republic of China on Taiwan" in the home page of its website. The same news media critics commented that these moves reflected the Taiwan independence ideology of the administration, and such efforts might restrict interactions with the mainland.[18]

Less than a year into his administration, President Chen was quoted as saying that "we will never be caught in the framework and trap of one China,"[19] in effect denying the government's position in 1992 that one China existed but could be differently interpreted. Although Chen had pledged that he would not abolish the NUC or abrogate its unification guidelines, he never convened the NUC and seems to have had no intention of doing so. In fact, he has informed the public that the NUC should not serve as a "totemic symbol" for Taiwan's people and blamed the GMD "for making the unification of China the only option" for Taiwan's future.[20] Chen's administration now tried to expunge the majority view of 1990–93 that Taiwan should engage the Mainland China

18. *World Journal*, March 1, 2002, p. A2.
19. Ibid.
20. *New York Times*, September 1, 2000, p. A3.

regime for long term reunification and instead promote Taiwanese nationalism and separate from China.

In the early 1980s the Taiwan Bankers' Association had posted a huge placard in front of the Office of the President containing the Chinese ideographs "Freedom and Democracy Will Unify China." Early in President Chen's administration that placard mysteriously disappeared. In March and May 2001 the Ministry of Defense ordered that any posters on its facilities that proclaimed "national unification" or "restore Chinese culture"—testimonials to former President Chiang Kai-shek—be removed. The Office of the President did not comment.

On October 10, 2001, the national birthday of the ROC, President Chen did not mention the divided China problem or how it could be resolved by negotiating a cooperative arrangement with the Beijing authorities based on a one-China principle. Instead, he appealed to Beijing's leaders to "abandon obsolete and rigid thinking, raise their intellectual horizon in facing cross-strait relations in the twenty-first century, and consider themes such as humanitarianism to overcome the present impasse between the two sides."[21]

President Chen's repeated appeals for negotiations with mainland China, if accepted by the Beijing authorities, would have meant their agreeing to the special state-to-state relationship that former President Lee had promoted. Beijing's authorities now perceived President Chen as a closet Taiwan nationalist and separatist like Lee Teng-hui. If they agreed to Chen's call for negotiations of all issues except the divided China problem, the two sides could talk endlessly without ever reaching an agreement. That strategy would enable President Chen to promote his revolution for establishing Taiwan independence. Moreover, if

21. "President Chen's National Day Message," *Taipei Journal* 18, no. 39 (October 12, 2001): 2.

negotiations continued long enough under Taipei's new rules, Taiwan nationalism would become the majority view and the Beijing authorities would lose all hope for China's peaceful reunification, leaving force as their only option. For these reasons, Beijing had refused negotiations with the Taipei authorities until both sides agreed to adopt the one China principle formula of 1992 that had made détente and negotiations possible.

After President Lee Teng-hui had abolished elections for the Taiwan Provincial Government's governor and assembly, the Chen government now planned to abolish village and township elections. Those elections, launched in 1950 to teach the people how to use the ballot box and practice self-governance, constituted an important experiment to implant the spirit of democracy. In place of these elections, the DPP would appoint party members to administer those communities. According to the government's revised "Act of Local Institutions," starting from 2006, the autonomous status and elections for village and township leaders were to be abolished, and village-township chiefs to be appointed by the county chief. The Ministry of the Interior justified this decision by claiming it would "save money, enhance efficiency, and eliminate local factions and 'black gold' [corrupt elements]." The opposition parties, led by the GMD, criticized this decision as a "setback for democracy" and an example of regime "white terror," but the DPP-ruled administration refused to budge.

Meanwhile, the Chen administration tried to gain control over the state-owned banks and industrial, transport, and utility corporations, just as the GMD had done when it held power. Fully aware of the DPP tactics, the opposition parties refused to bargain with administration officials. President Chen responded by calling their efforts mean-spirited and harmful to Taiwan and said their reluctance to work with him damaged Taiwan.

The new administration also expanded the teaching of Taiwanese language, culture, and history while downgrading Chinese culture and history. These policies, initiated by former President Lee, affirmed the primacy of Taiwan civilization, ignored China, and admired Japan's colonial rule of Taiwan. The Ministry of Education also printed new textbooks that emphasized Taiwan's history at the expense of China's and ordered public and private colleges to establish departments or institutes for the study of Taiwan literature. Minister of Education Ovid Tzeng made it very clear on October 15, 2001, that he would encourage all national universities to establish departments and graduate institutes of Taiwan history.[22]

The official language in Taiwan has been Chinese. To make it easier for Chinese and foreigners to learn the language, the Beijing government had publicized a "Chinese Phonetic Alphabet (Hanyu Pinyin)" in 1958. Later, this system was approved by the International Standard Organization (ISO) and the United Nations and adopted worldwide. The Taiwan authorities, however, wanted to promote a strong sense of being Taiwanese, and so they developed a "General Phonetic Alphabet (Tongyong Pinyin)" in 1998. After a year of experimenting, the educational authorities found it confusing, and decided to apply Hanyu Pinyin as phonetic symbols. Then in July 2002, the Ministry of Education ordered that Hanyu Pinyin be abandoned and to revert to Tongyong Pinyin. The Ministry also abolished the Act for Promoting Mandarin, approved during GMD rule and applied for decades. Many in leading educational and cultural circles saw these actions as politically and ideologically motivated to sever cultural ties with China. They argued that without the island's people using Mandarin as *the* common spoken language, how could the Taiwanese people communicate either with each other or with foreign countries?

22. Sandy Huang, "Tzeng Says Colleges Must Help Taiwanization Effort," *Taipei Times* 3, no. 124 (October 16, 2001): 2.

Japan's treatment of women during World War II has been criticized throughout East Asia and the world but not by the Chen administration. Two senior consultants of President Chen's, Hsu Wen-long and Chin Mei-ling, praised a cartoon book by the Japanese right-wing writer Yoshinori Kobayashi, but did not criticize its illustration that portrayed Taiwanese women as volunteering to serve as sexual companions of Japanese soldiers in order to help their social advancement. Moreover, Hsu and Chin repeatedly declared their admiration for Japanese colonial rule of Taiwan and strongly condemned the arrival of Nationalist troops and civil servants in 1945 as an "outside regime imposing colonial rule upon Taiwan." Their comments produced a great public furor, but president Chen defended Hsu and Chin by declaring that, because Taiwan was a democracy, he would "defend to the death the freedom of speech" of his two consultants and others to speak their minds freely.

The perception that the Chen administration favored a Taiwan Republic was reinforced by the red-carpet treatment it gave to a large conference in Taipei in March 2001, named the Congress of Taiwanese. Its participants called for creating a Republic of Taiwan and welcomed Chin Mei-ling as a hero. Some congress participants even took to the streets, shouting that Taiwan must be independent of China. President Chen attended the meeting and in his opening remarks declared that he was the elected president of Taiwan instead of the Republic of China. Then, the second annual meeting of the Congress of Taiwanese, held in Taipei on March 17, 2002, called for "rectifying the name of Taiwan," and "drawing up a state constitution." Some government leaders attended the meeting and pledged to "fight" for these goals. These developments show a new trend in Taiwan political life: the new governing party has chosen to promote Taiwan Nationalism as a new belief system, rather than the GMD-ruled administration's belief system that Taiwan is a part of China and China must be reunified.

Opposition party leaders have condemned President Chen's remarks and actions as politically irresponsible and socially divisive. Even the DPP former chairman Hsu Hsin-liang has urged President Chen to distance himself from the radical fundamentalists of his party who have long insisted that Taiwan is not part of China and must be allowed to form a new Taiwan nation state.

Chen Shui-Bian's Theory of "One Country on Each Side"

In early August of 2002, the mainland China authorities' top leaders gathered at the seaside resort of Beidahe to discuss the upcoming party congress and leadership succession. Meanwhile, on August 3rd, President Chen Shui-bian was speaking before a world body of pro-independence Taiwanese. Chen told them that "Taiwan and China, on each side of the Strait, are different countries." He had rejected China's fundamental position that both Taiwan and China are parts of the same country as well as the GMD's long standing commitment to reunifying mainland China and Taiwan.

Several days before, President Chen had spoken to a group of business leaders. He reiterated that Taiwan should stop having unrealistic expectations of China and that it must "go its own way." The "one China" principle and "one country, two systems," would mean a change of Taiwan's status quo that Taiwan's people could never accept, he said. Only 23 million Taiwanese people using the referendum, he continued, could determine whether the status quo situation on Taiwan should be changed. "I encourage everyone to seriously consider the importance and urgency of passing legislation for such a referendum."

President Chen had not even mentioned his "one country on

each side" formula to his three closest aides, the National Security Council secretary-general, Chiou I-jen, the head of the Mainland Affairs Council, Tsai Ing-wen, or premier, Yu Shyi-kun.[23] Government officials were surprised to hear his words, and some said they felt as if they had been hit on the head.[24]

From all of the above action and statements by the Chen administration, President Chen had broken his pledge, made in his inauguration speech, not to promote any referendum touching on the "independence" issue. The opposition parties and most of mass media condemned Chen's statement as violating his promises made before the presidential election, as well as his oath to the ROC constitution to uphold "one China." Chen's speech, as some commentators pointed out, essentially replaced Lee Teng-hui's "two states" formula in 1999.

Chen had subtly introduced the proposition that two states now existed, one on each side of the Taiwan Strait. His proposition differed from Lee's in that two states divided by the Taiwan strait had a "special relationship," but that relationship was never defined. Chen, however, was declaring that two sovereign, very different states and their peoples existed on separate sides of the Taiwan Strait. Chen's proposition now challenged mainland China's authorities to recognize a new reality.

President Chen's Remarks and the Reactions They Provoked Regarding Cross-Strait Relations since His Inauguration, May 15, 2000

Chen's statement was controversial, and a public opinion poll, conducted right after his speech, revealed that his support was at its lowest ebb, falling to 45.8 percent, compared with 80 percent

23. John Pomfret, "China and Taiwan Back Away from New Confrontation," *Washington Post*, August 10, 2002, p. A 14.
24. *World Journal*, August 5, 2002, p. A2.

when he became president in May 2000, and 50 percent on his first anniversary in office.[25] The great majority of Taiwanese still supported the status quo position of not challenging the basic rules that had allowed both regimes to peacefully co-exist. But Chen's new claim now worried the public.

For example, Chen's statement dealt a heavy blow to a weak Taiwan stock market, which lost 284 points on August 5, the biggest single day drop since November 11, 2001. Investors, who lost nearly 500 billion NT$ on that day, criticized President Chen for his irresponsible remark. Foreign investors, fearing a rising political risk premium, hastily withdrew increasisng amounts from Taiwan's stock market.

Beijing reacted predictably by warning Chen Shui-bian that his comments could cause a "disaster" and would seriously hurt ties between the two sides. For the first time Beijing mentioned Chen by name. Previously, it had called him the "Taiwan leader." One Chinese military source even said that although China strives for peaceful reunification, the justification to use military force to settle the Taiwan question is increased if Chen Shui-bian calls for a referendum on Taiwan's future.[26] A DPP official in the Mainland Affairs Council also admitted that Chen's remark had deepened the rift between the two sides and reduced the prospects for "three links" to take place any time soon.[27]

Chen's remarks also caught the U.S. government by surprise. According to some news reports, Douglas Paal, director of the American Institute on Taiwan (AIT), quickly met with President Chen and expressed the U.S. government's serious concern about his recent statement. Meanwhile, the U.S. ambassador to Beijing, Clark Randt, stated that Washington is extremely "unhappy" with

25. See 5, Pomfret.
26. *China Daily*, August 7, 2002, Print Edition.
27. *World Journal*, August 14, 2002, p. A2.

Chen's "one country on each side" statement, and reassured Beijing that the Bush administration's "one China" policy was unchanged.[28] To calm U.S. fears, Chen's government dispatched Premier Yu Shyi-kun and head of the Mainland Affairs Council, Tsai Ing-wen, to Washington to emphasize that Taiwan did not seek independence, nor did it reflect a change in policy toward mainland. A spokesman of the White House National Security Council responded that the U.S. wished to "take these statements at face value," and reiterated that the U.S. did not support Taiwan independence.[29] An American scholar called Chen's "one country on each side" policy a "very dangerous game" and one that could prove as counterproductive to Taiwan-U.S. relations as had been Lee Teng-hui's "state-to-state" comments. "Washington also needs to ask itself," he argued, if its policy of doing "whatever it takes" to help Taiwan defend itself is in the U.S. security interest.[30] Another Bush administration official commented that "if the U.S. arms sale to Taiwan and upgrading of the bilateral relations end up with the escalation of tensions in the Taiwan Strait, the U.S. may need to reevaluate its relationship with Taiwan.[31] Another American scholar wondered if Chen might abuse U.S. goodwill and get himself branded as a "troublemaker" in Washington's eyes.[32]

After weathering the storm, Chen's government officials then softened their remarks and played down the significance of Chen's statement. Officials repeatedly gave assurances that "to go its own way," as Chen had said, did not mean "independence,"

28. *World Journal*, August 7, 2002, p. A1; *United Daily News*, August 8, 2002, p. A1.

29. *World Journal*, August 8, p. A3, August 9, p. A3, 2002.

30. Ralph Cossa, "No Surprise?" *PacNet Newsletter* #31, Pacific Forum-Center for Strategic and International Studies, Washington DC, August 6, 2002.

31. *World Journal*, August 8, 2002, p. A3.

32. See 30 and 31.

and that his proposal of legislating a referendum was "a passive, defensive" measure, to prevent Beijing from changing the status quo. Both the government and DPP leaders reiterated that they would incorporate the DPP's "resolution regarding Taiwan's future" into the administration's mainland policy. This resolution, adopted by the DPP in 1999, had essentially stated that Taiwan was already a sovereign country called the "Republic of China," and that finally any change of the status quo must be determined by all of the people of Taiwan through referendum. Yet Chen's administration continued to reject the "one China" principle both sides had agreed upon in 1992.[33]

What motivated Chen to promote the "two states on each side" principle is not clear. Perhaps only those of his inner circle, like Chen Shimong, the Secretary-General of the Presidential office and an ardent Taiwan Nationalist, know. Maybe the Beijing authorities' actions to further isolate Taiwan by announcing that the tiny Pacific Ocean country of Nauru had just shifted diplomatic ties to Beijing, leaving only 27 countries officially recognizing Taiwan, had provoked Chen to make his remarks. Perhaps Chen believed the time was suitable to energize his base support for the March 2004 presidential elections. Maybe Chen even wanted to project his administration's confidence in order to garner financial support from Taiwan's business firms and win the next election.[34] Whatever the reasons, President Chen very likely hoped that Beijing's response would further anger Taiwan's people and elicit more popular support for his leadership and that perhaps the U.S. government's actions would elicit more popular support for his leadership.

33. *World Journal Weekly*, August 18, 2002, p. 4.
34. Richard Bush, "Cross-Strait Relations: A Time for Careful Management," *Brookings Northeast Asia Survey*, 2002–03, Brookings Institution, 2003, Washington DC, p. 71.

Whatever the reasons, President Chen had gambled that his remarks regarding Taiwan nationalism and separating from China would encourage more people to embrace that belief system. In this regard, he might have won.

5. Taiwan's Economic Slowdown and Growing Economic Integration with Mainland China

By late 2004, President Chen still had refused to resume cross-strait negotiations based on the "one China" consensus of 1992. But the opposition parties, the GMD, New Party (NP), and People First Party (PFP), supported that consensus. Yet the opposition had not offered a clear vision for Taiwan's future to connect with voters. Nor could the DPP and opposition parties agree on how to engage the Mainland China regime.

A new political party, the Taiwan Solidarity Union (TSU), had formed in 2001 and was vigorously supported by former President Lee and President Chen.[1] The TSU's chairman, former Minister of Interior Huang Chu-wen, announced that his party would support nearly forty candidates in the December 1, 2001, Legislative Yuan election. The TSU's manifesto proclaimed that it would "identify with Taiwan, devote itself to Taiwan and struggle for the future of Taiwan." The emergence of the TSU enabled former President Lee to reenter the political arena and bring with him some former GMD politicians. The GMD already had expelled Lee from the party after its defeat in March 2000.

GMD chairman Lien Chan and PFP leader James Soong still had not patched up their differences and united against the DPP. Many GMD elite distrusted Soong, and both Lien and Soong dis-

---

1. Catherine Hsieh, "New Taiwan Solidarity Union Gets Big-Name Support," *Taipei Journal* 18, no. 33 (August 24, 2001): 2.

agreed on the slate of candidates for the December 1, 2001, Legislative Yuan election as well as on the presidential and vice-presidential candidates for the March 2004 election. Nor could either leader articulate a vision for Taiwan's future.

Taiwan's Economic Depression

Taiwan's economy had deteriorated, mainly because of economic slowdown in the global economy. In the first quarter of 2001, Taiwan's economic growth rate fell by 0.09 percent; by August it had declined by 4.2 percent, with unemployment at an all-time high of 5.2 percent.[2] During 2001, manufacturing output fell and exports declined. Taiwan bank debt also increased, reaching a high of US$60 billion, or 20 percent of current gross domestic product. At the same time, as a result, consumer spending sharply declined, as did business investment, although the government spent NT$4 billion of public funds to reverse the stock market decline.[3] Not since the late 1940s had Taiwan's people felt so poor.

To address this slowdown, in August 2001 the Chen administration sponsored a three-day conference on Taiwan's economic relations with the mainland. Participants agreed that cross-strait economic relations must be expanded, but they could not agree on how to negotiate with Beijing to achieve that goal. The Mainland Affairs Council (MAC) could only recommend that "the government should quickly establish a consensus within the government, then work with the opposition to resolve differences over the 1992 consensus," and finally "consult with the mainland authorities to establish direct links and discuss other issues

2. Council for Economic Planning and Development, Executive Yuan of the Republic of China, *Industry of Free China* 91, no. 11 (November 2001): 74.
3. *World Journal* (in Chinese), March 19, 2001, p. A4.

related to the welfare of the people."[4] The government did not follow MAC's suggestion, because it was paralyzed.

After that economic conference, GDP declined by 2.1 percent in 2001. Private investment was stagnant, with consumer spending and demand sluggish. What worried the authorities most was the deteriorating investment environment. One leading poll showed 73.8 percent of the 1000 foreign companies' CEOs rating Taiwan's investment environment as "worsening," compared to only 21.9 percent in 1990. Moreover, 15.8 percent of the polled foreign CEOs intended to downsize or even withdraw their businesses from Taiwan.[5]

According to the Accounting Office of the Executive Yuan in 2002, the investment rate (share of investment in GDP) amounted to 17.3 percent, the lowest in 40 years, since 1963, when data was first collected. Taiwan's investment rate always had been above 20 percent. The report mentioned that although Japan suffered severe deflation, its investment rate was more than 24 percent. The figure was 26.7 percent for Korea, 24.1 percent for Singapore, and 38 percent for mainland China.[6] In the first half of 2002, labor unemployment climbed to 6.54 percent, a record high. According to a family wealth survey, the average net family assets in 2000 was $NT7.74 million and lower than in 1999, the first decline since this survey was conducted in 1988.[7] Another poll showed that over 71 percent of citizens saw no improvement in Taiwan's economy.[8]

As businessmen began to re-evaluate their strategy, they

4. Quoted from the summary report of the Mainland Affairs Division of the Economic Development Advisory Conference, "EDAC Outlines Cross-Strait Ties," *Taipei Journal* 17, no. 35 (September 7, 2001): 3.

5. *World Journal*, December 13, 2002, p. A8.

6. *World Journal*, August 19, 2002, p. A4.

7. *World Journal*, August 18, 2002, p. A7.

8. A public survey conducted by KMT, *World Journal*, August 6, 2002, p. A7.

blamed Chen's government for its poor economic performance saying "Its goals aren't clear, and the management team isn't experienced."[9] According to a survey of domestic companies, more than 60 percent were unsatisfied with government's management of the economy, and nearly 73 percent made the "three links" (direct trade, transportation, and communication) a "must" for the government's economic agenda. More executives now saw mainland China as their only salvation, and they were already moving their manufacturing to the mainland. With the global economy slump and Taiwan's economy deteriorating, many Taiwanese companies realized the mainland was not only a reliable manufacturing base, but a market for their products. They eagerly wanted to use the mainland's cheap pool of trained engineers and have access to its booming stock markets.

According to former President Lee's "no haste, be patient" rules, investment in the mainland still could not exceed US$ 50 million per project, and high-tech industries were not allowed to be constructed. Many companies found loopholes in the law and eventually forced the government to loosen its regulations. The DPP government officially dropped Lee's "no haste, be patient" policy and replaced it with "active opening and effective management." The government also expanded its list of industries and included some high-tech firms that could receive Taiwan investments.

These modest policy changes still did not satisfy the businesses that wanted direct trade, transportation, and communication with mainland China. Foreign companies in Taiwan, disappointed by the slow pace of the DPP authorities to approve direct cross-strait links, moved their industries to the mainland. United Parcel Services (UPS) moved its transfer center from the Chiang Kai-shek airport in Taiwan to Clark airport in the Philip-

9. *Business Week*, June 11, 2001, p. 57.

pines in April 2002, because Taiwan's embargo on direct transportation with the mainland prevented it from doing any business with the mainland. Another American company, Airis, also decided to withdraw from Taiwan and canceled a joint venture plan with Taiwan Sugar Company in Kaoshiung. Dell computers (Taiwan), the largest purchaser of information technology products in Taiwan, moved its Asia-Pacific purchasing headquarters from Taiwan to Hong Kong. Taiwan's media referred to these examples as the DPP's failure to promote "active opening, effective management" with the mainland. Douglas Paal, director of US AIT, expressed in late 2002 his concern about the delay of the "three links," pointing out that more than 100 foreign companies in Taiwan (60 percent were American), had moved to the mainland over the previous two years. He further opined that opening the "three links" would guarantee Taiwan's future rapid economic development, and that because without the "three links" Taiwan would become isolated and have no business opportunities.[10]

Just as labor-intensive industries depended on the mainland market, so did Taiwan's high technology industrial sector. Its high technology investment flows were increasing through Hong Kong, British Virgin Islands, and the U.S. to mainland China. According to Taiwan's official estimates, more than 50 percent of the information hardware production—computers, parts and peripherals, DVD, digital cameras—is made on the mainland. Taiwan's officials estimate that Taiwan's companies have invested nearly US$ 70 billion in China and are now operating more than 60,000 projects employing over a half a million expatriates. More than half of Taiwan's listed companies, and virtually all of the island's top conglomerates, have set up subsidiaries or joint ventures in the mainland, hoping to generate bigger revenues than in Taiwan.

10. *World Journal*, September 24, 2002, p. A2.

Cross-strait trade continues to thrive. Mainland China's share of Taiwan's total exports rapidly rose in the last decade and in 2002 surpassed the amount Taiwan exported to the U.S. for the first time. Mainland China now accounts for about 24.9 percent of Taiwan's total exports while the U.S. in 2003 remains Taiwan's number two trading partner in terms of total trade, albeit the U.S share of Taiwan's exports declined to 20.7 percent. From 1991 to the third quarter of 2002, Taiwan earned US$ 259 billion from its trade with the mainland (including Hong Kong).[11] Without trade with the mainland, Taiwan's international balance sheet would have run a large deficit.

As domestic economic prospects for Taiwan worsened and the mainland economy boomed, more small business owners and young professionals sought career opportunities in the mainland. Many even resettled with their families in Shanghai and other metropolitan areas. A public poll in 2002 found that at least one relative or friend works in the mainland for every three Taiwanese. Even popular opinion has shifted in favor of further economic integration with the mainland in 2002: 54 percent of those polled supported direct "three links."[12]

Although many complained that the DPP government has procrastinated in establishing the "three links," they were optimistic about the potential benefits for Taiwan's economy if direct links were opened:

- On average, over 300,000 Taiwanese travel to the mainland every year via Hong Kong. Should there be a direct flight between Taipei and Shanghai, each person would save 4–5 hours and Taiwan could save more than NT$ 50 billion annually.

11. Finance Ministry figures in Taipei, see *World Journal*, October 12, 2002, p. A8.
12. *World Journal*, July 12, 2002, p. A2.

- A small cargo ship sailing directly between Keelong and Shanghai, without stopping over in the Ryukyus and Japan as it does now, would save two days and 329 nautical miles. Taiwan's businessmen could reduce transportation costs by US$10 billion annually.

- Taiwan's civil airlines estimated the "three links" could bring business opportunities to Taiwan valued as high as NT$ 60 billion annually, to triple the current value of cross-strait transactions.

Political analysts and scholars have long pointed out that expediting the "three links" is the only solution for reducing Taiwan's current economic woes. Many blame the DPP authorities, claiming they are obsessed with ideology and winning votes while ignoring the mainland's expanding commercial opportunities.[13]

As Taiwan's polity fragmented and its economy declined, President Chen repeatedly talked about promoting better relations with the mainland authorities, but he publicly said those relationships must be based upon a state-to-state relationship. To be sure, Beijing wanted the "three links," but it always insisted that "domestic air and maritime" links cannot be conducted according to the "state-to-state" relationship as proposed by Chen's government. The Beijing authorities also suggested that airline and shipping companies on both sides of the Taiwan Strait should discuss how to promote the three links, but the Taiwan authorities always rejected their proposal.

Public opinion also has been volatile regarding relations between the two sides. A MAC public opinion poll in April 2002 revealed that popular support for the formula of "one country, two systems" had reached 16 percent, the highest in ten years.[14]

---

13. See the editorial, *World Journal*, October 12, 2002, p. A2.

14. *Renmin Ribao*, January 6, 1991, p. 1. Another poll, taken by *United Daily News* of the Taiwan area during June 25–27, 2001, reported that 33 percent

(In the past support had wavered between 5 and 9 percent.) The percentage of those respondents disliking the one-country, two-systems approach fell from 84 to 74 percent. Those favoring the status quo but amenable to a gradual move toward unification increased to 24 percent; those favoring the status quo but in favor of eventually moving toward independence declined to 18 percent. If we aggregate those opting for the one-country, two-systems approach with the pro status quo group agreeing to eventual unification, nearly one-half want to support direct negotiations under the one-China principle. But this falls far short of the national majority view in the early 1990s. The sentiments and beliefs of Taiwan's people dramatically changed after 1991.

Shelley Rigger, a professor of East Asian politics at Davidson College, contends that "while there are trends and forces propelling Taiwan towards closer ties with the mainland, there is little evidence that the key interests of the popular islanders cannot be met within the context of the status quo."[15] But if Taiwan nationalism and desire for independence increases and GMD political fragmentation continue to grow, the status quo opinion proportion is likely to contract. If the status quo contracts and Taiwan nationalism and independence grows, tensions between Taiwan and the mainland will increase.

Just as public opinion has shifted toward supporting Taiwan nationalism and independence, so too have election results reflected that change. On December 1, 2001, the DPP increased its Legislative Yuan seats from 70 to 87, and the new TSU party went from 0 to 13 seats, giving the two parties a total of 103 seats

---

accepted the "one country, two systems" formula (it was higher if "China," signifying one country, was the ROC). A similar poll in 2000 reported only 18 percent accepted the "one country, two systems" formula.

15. Shelley Rigger, "Maintaining the Status Quo: What It Means, and Why the Taiwanese Prefer It," *Cambridge Review of International Affairs* 14, no. 2 (April 2001): 112.

and 45.1 percent of the vote. The GMD-controlled seats declined from 110 to 68, the NP seats declined from 8 to 1, and the PFP, led by James Soong, increased its seats from 20 to 46 for a total of 115 seats (54.5 percent of the vote). A few years before, the DPP struggled to transcend the ceiling of 30 percent of the popular vote, but in 2001 it could count on around 40 percent. The two parties (DPP and TSU) favoring Taiwan independence still fell short of the Legislative Yuan majority of 113 seats. There is also no guarantee that the three parties, whose members formerly belonged to the GMD, will vote their 115 seats as a bloc. The DPP and TSU alliance could obtain support from the ten independent candidates who won ten seats in the Legislative Yuan, some of whom had defected from other parties. Political bargaining behind the scenes has already increased.

Beijing's New Overtures toward Taiwan

Ever since the PRC's Premier Zhu Ronji's finger-wagging T.V. appearance in early 2000, warning Taiwan's people to vote correctly, China's leaders have adopted a low profile and merely observed President Chen's activities without comment. But at the same time, the Beijing authorities were offering the Taiwan authorities new options to promote more cooperation between the two sides in order to jump-start negotiations. In two decisive ways the PRC regime had compromised.

Beijing's Flexibility regarding the "Three Links" Issue

As Taiwan's economy continued to slow down, the "three-links" issue became more important for Taiwan. Beijing insisted that both sides send representatives to talk about the "three links" under the "One China" principle. Taiwan refused. Beijing then redefined the "three links" to be "the internal affair of one country," stipulating that air and sea traffic across the strait constituted a "special domestic line," and that there need not be any mention of "One China." Beijing also proposed that both governments authorize private air and shipping associations to represent both sides and negotiate agreements acceptable to their respective civil air and maritime authorities. This arrangement seemed to have trumped all other jurisdiction issues. As the PRC's Qian Qichen put it: although there are political differences between the two sides, cross-strait negotiations and the "three links" are not the same thing. The latter can be negotiated by civil organizations, just as was done in the 2002 airline talks between Taiwan and Hong Kong. According to the Office of Taiwan affairs, defining the "three links" as "the internal affair of one country" protected and ensured the rights of both sides to navigate, trade, and fish in their neighboring maritime waters.

The foreign media praised Beijing's new stand. "The ball now is in Chen Shui-bian's court," said a commentary in *The Wall Street Journal*. "If Chen can grab this opportunity and promote the 'three links' as soon as possible instead of deferring it until after the 2004 election, it will be beneficial for Taiwan's economic recovery and cross-strait peace for several years."[16] But Chen refused Beijing's new offer. Less than a month later, he proclaimed the "one country on each side" thesis, even after Beijing repeated that the door was still open to discuss the "three links" issue.

In October 2002, Qian Qichen, in an interview with Taiwan journalists, made another concession. He said that the "three links" is an economic issue rather than a political one. There is no precondition that Taiwan should first accept "One China." He continued that the "three links" constituted a special track to connect the two sides of the strait; the mainland did not insist upon

16. See *The Wall Street Journal*, July 8, 2002, Online Edition.

a "special domestic line." Ships entering the port of the other side need not hoist any official flag except its own company's flag. "It's their own business what flags they want to have in the high sea." "As for air flights, as soon as the airline officials of both sides sit down and talk, everything can easily be resolved." Qian later added that political differences should not prevent economic cooperation.

The Taiwan media described Beijing's new move as flexible and friendly, because it substituted "cross-strait links" for "special domestic line," thus depoliticizing the "three links."[17] But President Chen rejected Beijing's new overture; and told the media that the people should understand the "three links" is not a "panacea" to solve all of Taiwan's economic problems.[18]

Beijing Redefines Its "One China" Principle

Meanwhile, the Beijing authorities offered Taipei's leaders the same "one China" concept advocated by the Taiwan authorities in 1992. In July 2000, Vice Premier Qian Qichen told a group of Taiwan journalists that "one China" is "not exclusive"; but he later told a delegation from Taiwan's *United Daily News* that "the common divisor on both sides of the strait is 'one China.' Even the Taiwan Guidelines for National Unification had affirmed that view. One China does not mean the PRC." He continued, "Both the Mainland and Taiwan together make up one China." Qian repeated this interpretation at the National People's Congress on March 9, 2001, and again at the Asia Society in New York on March 21, 2001. The Taiwan authorities never officially responded to Beijing's new offer, believing it to be insincere.

Beijing again modified the connotation of the "one China" principle at a reception for the 10th anniversary of the founding

17. *World Journal*, October 17, 2002, p. A3.
18. *World Journal*, October 23, 2002, p. A2.

of ARATS on December 16, 2001. As Chen Yunlin, director of the Taiwan Affairs Office, stated it, there is only one China in the world. Both mainland and Taiwan belong to that one China. The sovereignty and territorial integrity of China is inalienable. Wang Daohan, Chairman of ARATS, also pointed out that the "1992 Consensus" can be explicated as "both mainland and Taiwan belong to one China." He then said that once the Taiwan authorities accept the "1992 Consensus," ARATS is ready to conduct dialogue and negotiation with SEF.

Beijing further softened its position toward Taiwan at a ceremony commemorating the 7th anniversary of Jiang Zemin's Eight-Point Proposal. Qian Qichen also welcomed members of the DPP to visit China and called for renewed dialogue and stronger economic ties across the strait. "We believe there is a distinction between the vast majority of DPP members and a very small number of stubborn Taiwan independence activists," he said, "We invite them to tour mainland China and visit by appropriate status to promote understanding." Taiwan experts in Beijing praised this move because Beijing would now be directly dealing with the DPP.[19] In Taiwan, about 67 percent of respondents of a public poll endorsed Beijing's new overture and judged it to be based on goodwill.[20] The U.S. media also stated that Qian's new gesture showed that Beijing was more confident in understanding the aspirations of the Taiwanese to run their own affairs.[21]

In the past, Taiwan's authorities had complained that Beijing ignored the existence of the ROC. Tang Shubei, the former vice chairman of ARATS, and now director of the Research Center of Cross Strait Relations, offered the following candid, bold interpretation. Both the ROC and PRC, he stated in San Francisco on

19. *Washington Post*, January 24, 2002, Online Edition.
20. *World Journal*, January 28, 2002, p. A2.
21. *The Wall Street Journal*, January 30, 2002, p. A18.

August 31, 2002, are political symbols that constitute an obstacle to reunification and should not be taken too seriously. What should be emphasized, he argued, is that both sides of the strait belong to one country. He urged that an agreement be signed by the two sides "that Taiwan rejects independence and the mainland rejects the use of force."[22] The 16th CCP Congress in November 2002 also called for an early resumption of cross-strait dialogue and negotiation. In his political report to the Congress, Jiang Zemin specified that, under the premise of the one China principle, the following issues can be discussed: formally ending hostility between the two sides; Taiwan's international activities regarding economic, cultural, and social affairs, and the political status of Taiwan authorities.[23] This is the first time that Beijing officially acknowledged that it was willing to address Taiwan's demand for a greater role in the international order.

President Chen refused to reply to any of these overtures, and he repeatedly said he would not conduct cross-strait talks under any one China premise. Wang Daohan again appealed to Taiwan on the occasion of the 10th anniversary of Koo-Wang talks. "There never has been dialogues and negotiations in history without a common foundation and some designated goals," he stated, and the "1992 consensus is a historical fact." Beijing, Wang said, is willing to fully respect Taiwan's views and suggestions and will never demand more than what is contained in the 1992 consensus. So far, all of Beijing's offers have not elicited any response from the DPP government.

By refusing to acknowledge the 1992 "one China" consensus, the Taiwan authorities had slammed shut the door that would

22. *World Journal*, September 1, 2002, p. B1.

23. Jiang Zemin, *Quanmian Jianse Xiaokang Shehui, Kaichuan Zhongguo Tese Shehuizuyi Shiye Xinjumian*, (Completely Building a well-off society: Opening a New Phase of Socialism with Chinese Characteristics), Report to the 16th National Congress of CCP, People's Publishing House, Beijing, 2002, p. 45.

open up both sides to negotiate. President Chen Shui-bian certainly knew that. Yet he continued to make overtures to the Mainland China authorities to negotiate a resolution of the divided China, always denying the existence of the 1992 "one China" consensus. A stand-off had been reached, and the new DPP-led government continued its policy of de-Sinification and promoting Taiwan independence.

6. The Watershed Elections of 2004 and Aftermath

On March 20, 2004, voters went to the polls to cast their votes for either incumbent President Chen Shui-bian and Annette Lu, vice-presidential candidate, or the GMD ticket—chairman Lien Chan and his vice presidential candidate PFP chairman James Soong. The parties had been preparing for this great political battle for more than six months. During the long campaign, economic conditions did not significantly improve. Polls repeatedly showed that the new political alliance of the GMD, NP, and PFP was slightly ahead by four to six percentage points.

According to a late December 2003 public poll conducted in Taiwan by the U.S. Department of State, 75 percent of the respondents worried most about the economy.[1] Since the DPP had won political power in 2000, Taiwan's "economic miracle" had been fading because of the worst economic recession since 1949.

Although President Chen came up with a slogan of "fighting the economy *(pin jingji)*" in June 2001, and his administration had built some infrastructure and technology-scientific parks, macroeconomic conditions had not improved. In 2001 the economic recession eased, but GDP only rose by 3.5 percent in 2003. (Recall that the average annual GDP growth rate during 50 years of GMD rule had been 8.1 percent).[2] Private consumer spending in 2002 only rose by 1.9 percent, compared to the annual average

---

1. *World Journal*, December 21, 2003, p. A9.
2. Su Chi, *Brinkmanship: From Two-States-Theory To One-Country-on-Each-Side* (Taipei: Commonwealth Publishing Group, 2003), p. 249.

growth rate of more than 5 percent during GMD rule. At the same time, the unemployment rate reached a record high of 5.2 percent.[3] General Accounting Office (GAO) data showed that even if the forecasted GDP per capita in 2004 could reach US$13,771, this target barely matched the level of 2000. According to a World Economic Forum worldwide survey in 2002, 68 percent of respondents in Taiwan said they were not as well off as ten years earlier. Between 2000 and 2003, domestic private investment declined from $1.55 trillion NT (US$ 46.9 billion) to $1.08 trillion NT (US$ 32.7 billion). The overall investment rate had plunged by 20 percent in 2003, a record low.[4] Even worse, foreign investment was recorded at US$ 1.44 billion in 2002, compared to US$ 4.1 billion in 2001 and US$ 4.9 billion in 2000.[5]

Businesspeople and scholars blamed the DPP administration for poor management of the economy and dismissed the "fighting the economy" slogan as a joke. The Fourth Nuclear Plant, already half constructed, had to halt work. Then the administration decided to complete the project, and work resumed. What disappointed businesspeople most was the government's vacillating policies.

The DPP administration tenaciously refused to promote the "three links" for direct communication and transportation as described in the last chapter; thus, the potential for expanding trade, investment and people exchange between the two sides was never realized. More foreign airlines suspended their direct flights from America and Europe to Taipei, and redirected their businesses to Shanghai and Shenzhen.[6] Many businesspeople pleaded with Taiwan's authorities to make cross-strait relations a top priority in the next administration.

3. Ibid., p. 250.
4. Ibid.
5. *World Journal*, September 5, 2003, p. A5.
6. *World Journal*, September 29, 2003, p. A8.

The Election Issues

Because the Chen government had not been able to revive the economy, the pan-blue's presidential candidates, Lien Chan and James Soong, consistently ran ahead in the polls by around ten percentage points in the first half of 2003. Meanwhile, political commentators ruminated that, because of unfavorable economic circumstances, Chen might base his campaign on the popular position of improving cross-strait relations by direct air and sea links. But, President Chen refused this course because he had never accepted the compromises offered by the Beijing authorities. A new election issue now took center stage.

In May 2003, the World Health Organization (WHO), under pressure from the PRC, denied Taiwan's request to join that organization as an observer. President Chen quickly reacted by instructing his administration to hold a public referendum on whether Taiwan should join the WHO. Chen also proposed that his administration hold two referendums with the presidential election on March 20, 2004: (1) Should Taiwan enter the WHO, and (2) should the plan for constructing the Fourth Nuclear Plant be continued? Chen said that these referendums would be held according to his new principle that there was "one country on each side" of the Taiwan Strait. Chen had now found a major issue to differentiate the DPP alliance from the GMD alliances for the upcoming presidential election. He would campaign on the issue of Taiwan's right to have election referendums.

Political analysts in Taipei observed that while Chen trailed behind his opponents in opinion surveys, he now tried to shift voters' attention from economics to politics. Because an island-wide consensus wanted Taiwan to enter WHO, Chen proposed this referendum, knowing Beijing would oppose it and that that would make Taiwan's people angry. Chen was appealing to the ideology of democracy to argue that the "referendum was a universal value and a basic right of the people." If Chen could obtain popular approval for his referendum, he could stage other referendums to revise the constitution, change the country's name, etc., thus legitimizing Taiwan's de facto independent state when conducting the future election of 2008.[7] Chen's strategy seemed to be working, because several polls in the second half of 2003 showed that he had narrowed the gap with Lien Chan to just a few percentage points.

Many scholars have argued that the referendum is not necessary for legitimating democracy. In ancient Greece, a referendum was held almost once a month in the city-state of Athens, and not surprisingly, most pro-independence Taiwanese have interpreted democracy as majority rule and holding referendums as appropriate. History has shown, however, that this practice has major drawbacks. First, the will of even an exceedingly small majority can nullify the minority's will, which is not a suitable standard of fairness if each side has tried to mislead the other. Second, for there to be justice, government must be neutral, but that is difficult to implement in practice. Third, not all citizens possess sufficient information about key issues, and they often vote according to poor information. For these reasons, using the referendum has been limited in modern democracies.

The Charter of the United Nations states that not all peoples have the right of "independence through referendum." Self-determination is the right of autonomy, not the right of secession, and it is given only to those non-dominion and trust territories that want to abolish colonial domination. After Quebec's referendum in 1995, the Supreme Court of Canada ruled in 1998 that Quebec is obligated to enter into negotiations with the federal government and other provinces if it intends to pursue independence. Without

7. Willy Wo-Lap Lam, "Referendum Stirs up Taiwan Strait," CNN.com Hong Kong, August 19, 2003.

federal government approval, Quebec's unilateral announcement of independence was deemed invalid. In March of 2000, a new law in Canada further stipulated that any referendum for independence by Quebec first must be approved by the federal government.[8]

President Chen said he would authorize the Executive Yuan to order a referendum at the same time the election was to be held on March 20, 2004. According to the ROC constitution, citizens have the rights of initiative and referendum. But exercising these two rights must be determined by the law, which calls for first exercising these two rights in half of the nation's cities and counties. The president and executive branch have no authority to initiate a referendum. Taiwan's opposition parties now condemned Chen's wish to hold a referendum as violating the constitution and the Law of Administrative Procedures.[9]

Strong opposition from Beijing and Washington finally forced President Chen to abandon his demand that the Executive Yuan initiate a referendum and that the Legislative Yuan then approve a referendum bill. Meanwhile, Chen's rise in the polls caused the pan-blue coalition to change its campaign strategy. Instead of publicly rejecting the referendum bill, the pan-blue coalition endorsed it. After heated debate, partly caused by new concerns from Washington, the Legislative Yuan passed the pan-blue's proposed version of the bill on November 27, 2003. It included some tough standards for ensuring passage and prohibited the executive branch from initiating any referendum. It now seemed that Chen might have no chance to initiate a referendum by March 2004. But a loophole in the bill was discovered and that enabled Chen to interfere once again.

8. "The Myth of Referendum," *World Journal*, September 4, 2002, p. B2; and Yan Jiaqi, "Nine Points on Referendum," *World Journal Weekly*, February 8, 2004, p. 30–32.

9. *World Journal*, June 25, 2003, p. A6.

The new law's Article 17 stipulated that the President could call a "defensive referendum if the sovereignty of the ROC were threatened." Several days later, Chen announced that because the PRC had deployed missiles in its coastal provinces and aimed them at Taiwan, the defensive referendum clause gave him the power to hold referendums concurrently with the upcoming presidential election on March. 20, 2004.

Beijing's leaders strongly criticized Chen when Chinese Premier Wen Jiabao visited the U.S. in November of 2003. Not long after meeting with the Premier, President George W. Bush finally intervened by stating that his government opposed any form of referendum that would unilaterally change the status quo of Taiwan. Now pressured from Washington and Beijing, the Legislative Yuan adopted on January 16, 2004, a watered-down referendum unlike that which Chen had originally envisaged. His "peace referendum" on March 20 posed the following two related issues.

"We, the people of Taiwan demand that the Taiwan Strait issue be resolved through peaceful means. Should mainland China refuse to withdraw its missiles that are targeted at Taiwan and openly renounce the use of force against us, would you agree that the government should acquire more advanced anti-missile weapons to strengthen Taiwan's self-defense capabilities?" The other referendum asked: "Do you agree that our government should negotiate with mainland China a 'peace and stability' framework for cross-strait interactions in order to build consensus and expand the welfare of the peoples on both sides of the Taiwan Strait?"

Opposition coalition members, legal experts, and even some leading members of the DPP denounced Chen for distorting Article 17 of the Referendum Law. Three retired grand justices and two constitutional scholars pointed out that Article 17 was an emergency clause that contained the "defensive referendum" concept which was to be used when there was a "threat to the state from outside" and the "danger of a change in sovereignty." At this time, however, there was no immediate threat to Taiwan because missiles had been stationed across the strait for many years. If there was any "threat," the presidential election should have been called off. The emergency power of the ROC president is not unlimited. Before exercising power, the president must address the "Referendum Review Committee," which was to be established by the Legislative Yuan. But Chen had produced this referendum without consulting anyone. To combine a presidential election with a "defensive referendum" also undermined the separation of powers and constitutional checks-and-balances. From all of the above, Chen's referendum also undermined Taiwan's democracy and the rule of law.[10]

The two questions contained in the proposed referendum did not relate to any immediate threats toward the ROC's democracy. Nobody in Taiwan would oppose "strengthening self-defense" and a policy to "engage in negotiation with mainland China." Some U.S. officials also said that a democratic society usually initiates referendums only to resolve controversial issues. They further opined that "we are highly suspicious about the motivation behind the proposed referendum."[11] With the election looming, and Chen's popular approval only slightly rising after the pan-blue coalition had formed, he was fighting a tough battle to be re-elected. Early 2004 polls had revealed him to be lagging behind his opponents. Chen had nothing to lose by promoting a referendum, and if that angered China and won him support from independence-minded voters, Chen believed he might win the March 2004 presidential election.

Mainland Chinese officials then responded that if Taiwan's

10. *World Journal*, February 17, 2004, p. A2.
11. Interview given by U.S. Deputy Assistant Secretary of State, Randall Schriver to Phoenix TV Station of Hong Kong in Shanghai, chinesenews net.com, February 3, 2004.

leadership held their referendum, that could cause a war. Meanwhile, ignoring Beijing's threat and strong disapproval by the United States, Japan, and some major European countries, President Chen still pressed ahead with his plan to hold the referendum on voting day, March 20. Opposition leaders continued to denounce Chen's tactic as illegal and called for voters to boycott it. The Law of Referendum also stated that if fewer than 50 percent of the electorate voted for the referendum, it would be invalidated.

But Chen's new proposal worried many because he seemed intent on drafting a new constitution, even if that required using the referendum to justify such action. His political position was that Taiwan was already an independent sovereign state that was not part of China. If this political development, as our narrative has argued, was affirmed by reforming the 1948 ROC Constitution, that would enrage mainland China and produce a conflict across the Taiwan Strait. Washington now responded to Chen's declaration by authorizing a Department of State spokesman to describe Chen's initiative as "election rhetoric" and to remind President Chen not to abandon his "Four No's plus One Without (*si bu, yi meiyou bu*)" pledge made in his inaugural speech on May 20, 2000.

In that pledge Chen had vowed the following: not to declare Taiwan independence; not to change the nation's name from "Republic of China" to "Republic of Taiwan"; not to include the special state-to-state relations thesis in the constitution; and not to promote a referendum for unification or independence. Chen also had pledged not to abolish the National Unification Council and its guidelines for national unification, yet he had never followed those guidelines and used the Council as originally designed.

Chen later reassured the U.S. government that he had not abandoned his pledge, and the U.S. government responded by saying "it appreciated Chen's pledge and takes it very seriously." These exchanges reassured Chen of American support for his administration if only he could find some way to revise the constitution without violating his pledge.

As for Chen's referendums regarding the new constitution, some high-ranking DPP members publicly reminded Chen to be cautious in promoting his initiatives. Facing pressure from both Washington and the DPP, Chen began modifying his previous statements, saying that the new constitution would have to be approved by the people through referendum, and that a proposed new constitution did not imply changing the country's name, national anthem, or proclaiming independence from China. But Chieu I-jen, secretary-general of the presidential office, later said he would not exclude the possibility of making these changes in the future.[12]

The March 20, 2004, Presidential Election

The Taiwan economy began to pick up steam in early 2004, but cross-strait political relations were stalemated. Chen's pan-green coalition continued to trail the pan-blue coalition in the polls. Just a week before the March 20, 2004 election, polls showed the pan-blue coalition leading by 6–8 points. Meanwhile, the contest had heated-up with the two sides and their supporters attacking each other. The discussions regarding ethnicity and political party differences became more acrimonious. The American China expert Kenneth Lieberthal described Taiwan's rising political temperature as a political event in which "Identity politics are rarely pragmatic—and rarely stoppable."[13] Lee Teng-hui and President Chen revived the February 28th tragedy theme by organizing the "hands across Taiwan" event on February 28th. The DPP and

12. *World Journal*, October 3, 2003, p. A5.
13. *New York Times*, March 3, 2004, p. A4.

TSU succeeded in mobilizing more than a million people to form a "human chain," while shouting slogans like "Taiwan yes, China no" and "love Taiwan by referendum." The race still was too close to call, anti-mainland sentiment became more vitriolic, and demands for an independent, Republic of Taiwan resounded throughout the island.

The ROC's 11th presidential and vice-presidential election was held peacefully on March 20, 2004. The Chen-Lu team received 29,518 more votes than the Lien-Soong ticket carrying the day by a razor-thin margin of only 0.22 percent. On March 21st, the Central Election Commission declared that Chen and Lu had won the election. Lien and Soong immediately called for a court-supervised recount and filed a lawsuit to annul the election on the grounds of too many irregularities at the polls. Although Lien and Soong had been defeated, the referendums that had caused so much furor failed to obtain the 50 percent voter participation and were defeated. While 90.3 percent of eligible voters voted to elect a president and running mate, only 45 percent voted for the two referendums. The pan-blue coalition had appealed to voters to abstain from voting for the referendums, but the voters had not elected Lien and Soong, even though they had led in the polls for more than four months! Why?

It had been reported in mid afternoon on Friday, March 19, that a bullet had grazed Chen's lower abdomen and Vice-President Lu's right knee when they rode in an open-air jeep motorcade tour through Tainan city. No one was arrested. No one saw the shooting. And no one pursued the alleged killers. News of the alleged political assassination spread across the island like a wild fire.

Pan-blue spokesmen asserted the shooting incident might have been staged to encourage voters to support President Chen. Although an ineffective security force protected the president and vice-president, Chen and Lu had not worn bulletproof vests.

Nobody on the street heard the shots being fired because fire crackers were being exploded. Chen had been taken to a hospital, far from the shooting, and not the hospital designated by the presidential guards in case of an emergency. GMD spokesman Su Chi reminded the nation that when running for office eighteen years ago, Chen appeared at a rally with an intravenous drip and claimed that he had been poisoned by the GMD. Yet he appeared healthy the next day. Mr. Su declared that the poisoning affair had been an election gambit to win voters' sympathy.[14]

Many reporters stated that the pan-green alliance might have staged the assassination to win sympathy votes. Reports immediately after the shooting announced that pro-DPP underground radio stations in central and southern Taiwan had spread the news that "Lien-Soong were cooperating with Communist China and had hired an assassin to kill Chen and Lu."[15]

Although this strange affair did not imply any criminal behavior, roughly a million voters had very likely transferred their votes to Chen and his vice-president because of these events. Another controversy erupted about the president and government putting the nation on emergency alert, thus preventing as many as 200,000 military and police personnel from voting. Taiwan lacked an absentee voting system. By a miracle the DPP had "bagged" an election that by all appearances it had seemed likely to lose.

The pan-blue coalition immediately launched legal challenges to the election results. It also rejected Chen's victory by alluding to huge counting errors. The Central Election Commission later admitted that 337,297 ballots were invalid—more than eleven times Chen's small victory margin and nearly three times as many as in previous presidential elections. The pan-blue coalition also claimed ballot box fraud. Crowds demonstrated in Taipei's streets

14. "Taiwan's Leader Wins Vote; Tally is Disputed," *New York Times*, March 21, 2004, online edition.

15. *World Journal*, April 20, 2004, p. A6.

for roughly a week after the election to protest that an unfair election had taken place.

On July 23, 2004 the blue alliance legal team reported five types of irregular voting results from recount findings held under court supervision.[16] These irregularities appeared in 9,777 voting precincts or 71.1 percent of all voting precincts. Other statistical measures also showed that most irregularities occurred in central and southern Taiwan in places such as Changhwa, Pingtung, Yunlin, and Chiayi counties, Tainan and Kaohsiung cities, stronghold areas supportive of the DPP. Moreover, irregular voter registers were found in 13,259 voting precincts or 96.44 percent of all precincts.

On July 21st the Chairperson of the Research and Planning Commission of the Ministry of Foreign Affairs, Ms. Yang Huang May-hsing, reported to the Ministry's posts in foreign countries that she was 99.9 percent certain that the "legal process now under way would not change the result of the March 20 election." She proved to be correct when in the fall of 2004 the ROC judiciary ruled that the election results could not be overturned

The December 2004 Legislative Yuan Election and Aftermath

In his May 20, 2004 inauguration speech, President Chen promised that his party would "lead the way in addressing such issues" as identity and ethnicity.[17] He emphasized that in the past "members of all ethnic groups have been victimized" by the GMD controlled authoritarian government. Chen appealed to the people to unite, support reform, and achieve his administration's goals.

The president now stressed that his primary goal was to

16. *Legal Team Reports on Recount Findings*, Press Release, Lien-Soong Campaign Headquarters, July 23, 2004.

17. *http://www.taipeitimes.com/News/from/archives/2004/05/20/2003 15631*.

reform the ROC Constitution. Because consensus did not exist regarding "national sovereignty, territory and the subject of unification/independence," he promised to abide by the following rules outlined in the constitution:

> Accordingly, after the passage by the national legislature, members of the first and also the last Ad Hoc National Assembly will be elected and charged with the task of adopting the constitutional reform proposal as passed by the legislature, abolishing the National Assembly, and incorporating into the Constitution the people's right to referendum on constitutional revision.

This would not be an easy task. To amend the ROC Constitution required a proposal endorsed by one-fourth of the Legislative Yuan members. Any constitutional amendment change must then be supported by three-fourths of the members present—at which time there must be a quorum of three-fourths of the Yuan's members. These stringent rules were part of the reason why the two grand coalitions began preparing as early as the summer of 2004 for the December 2004 Legislative Yuan election. Whichever coalition garnered the most Legislative Yuan seats had the best chance of initiating or blocking constitutional change.

In his acceptance speech President Chen also reminded Taiwan's people of his 'middle road' approach which the administration had adopted to reform Taiwan's polity and to build bridges of peace to the PRC. He insisted that his presidential duty was to "defend the sovereignty, security and dignity of the nation" and he promised to establish a "Committee for Cross-Strait Peace and Development" that would combine "the collective insight and wisdom of all parties and our citizenry," and to draft the "Guidelines for Cross-Strait Peace and Development" which would "pave the way for formulating a new relationship of cross-strait peace, stability and sustainable development." President Chen's directives were similar to those he had made four years before.

As our narrative has repeatedly asserted, the Beijing authorities will not approve of President Chen's committee's work if President Chen does not abandon his principle that separate sovereign states already exist across the Taiwan Strait. The Beijing authorities believe that Taiwan is part of China and that Chen's theory violates the 1992 "one China" principle consensus. A clear pattern has emerged. If Chen tries to reform the constitution, Beijing's leaders will threaten force.

In July 2004 President Chen again informed Taiwan's people that "the policy of the United States toward Taiwan will not be altered by the result of the November presidential election in the U.S.," and, he firmly defended his administration's plan to purchase NT$610.8 billion of defensive armaments from Washington.[18] He justified this expenditure over a fifteen year period by asking "If we do not have a minimum deterrence capability, how can we deter war?" When questioned about the failed shooting attempt on the day before the election, Chen declared: "we did not stage this shooting, so we have nothing to fear from an investigation." The Chen administration had every intention of expanding Taiwan's weaponry whereas the blue coalition had opposed such actions in the Legislative Yuan.

When Premier Yu Shyi-kun delivered his June 1, 2004 report to the Legislative Yuan outlining the administration's goals for the next four years, he first stressed "developing a national consciousness to promote ethnic harmony in a pluralistic society," then cited the resolution of social problems such as care for the elderly, and strengthening international competitiveness.[19] He never mentioned how Taiwan's economy might be restructured to have advanced services and become integrated with the market economies of other nations in the Asia-Pacific region, especially main-

18. *Taiwan News*, July 30, 2004, p. 1.
19. *Taiwan Journal*, Vol. XX1, No. 24, June 18, 2004, p. 1.

land China. The Chen administration had abandoned the government's 1990s economic strategy of upgrading Taiwan's services.

Meanwhile, non-governmental organizations like *The Alliance to Campaign for Rectifying the Name of Taiwan* had agreed upon a new strategy. Peter Wang, executive director of this organization, stated in early August 2004, that instead of overtly campaigning for changing Taiwan's status, "we haven't changed our ultimate goal to have this country's name changed to Taiwan. But before we can achieve this goal, it is more important to forge a national consensus among everyone living in Taiwan to identify with this place."[20]

Such private activities for new nation building meshed with the DPP's leaders' demand that society's celebrities toe its ideological line or else. After Taiwan's top pop diva Chang Hui-mei, or A-Mei, gave a concert in Beijing in July 2004, vice-president Annette Lu on August 6, 2004 stated in a radio station interview: "If a war breaks out between the two sides, I want to know whether she will go ahead with singing in Beijing, or choose to safeguard the island's 23 million people . . . Which one is more important for her?"[21] The pattern of intimidating individuals perceived as opposing Taiwan nationalism was becoming commonplace in the second term Chen administration.

In October, Taiwan's economy was gradually improving, as unemployment fell to 4.3 percent.[22] For many months candidates from the DPP and GMD coalitions had been preparing for a ferocious election battle on December 10, 2004 for seats in the Legislative Yuan. Polls showed the DPP coalition running slightly ahead in the election race.

20. *Taipei Times*, August 6, 2004, p. 3.
21. Keith Bradshaw, "Taiwan Watches Its Economy Slip to China" *New York Times*, December 13, 2004.
22. *http://taiwansecurity.org/AFP/2004/AFP-061204.htm.*

President Chen promised on December 6, 2004 that he would increase the use of "Taiwan" rather than Taiwan's official designation of ROC, but that he would not change the national title of the ROC, because it "not only reflects the reality but also is something that can be agreed upon by people of different ideologies under the present circumstances."[23] Again President Chen was promoting Taiwan nationalism by minimizing official usage of ROC. President Chen also announced that the government would remove the term 'China' from all state-controlled firms and include the word 'Taiwan' in all Taiwanese missions abroad.

Nor had President Chen ceased his criticism of all things Chinese in Taiwan. In early November 2004 he had labeled Dr. Sun Yat-sen, the father of modern China, as a 'foreigner' in Taiwan, ignoring the fact that education texts in Taiwan's elementary schools referred to Dr. Sun repeatedly. In late November, President Chen promised his government "would terminate" the "Chinese constitution" that had created "four major phenomena of chaos" in Taiwan.[24] On November 27, 2004 the Ministry of Education reported that classical Chinese works would make up only half the curriculum in Chinese-language courses, down from the current two-thirds, and that Chinese would be taught only four days a week instead of five.[25]

President Chen, on November 25, 2004, also declared that his DPP government would strive to enter the United Nations under the name of "Taiwan" in order to secure the representation rights of the 23 million Taiwanese people.[26] All of the above were President Chen's frenetic activities in the few weeks before election day to strengthen his base of Taiwan nationalist—independent voters to support the DPP and its ally the TSU.

---

23. *http://taiwansecurity.org/CP/2004/CP-281104.htm.*
24. *http://taiwansecurity.org/News/2004/UPI-271104.htm.*
25. *http://taiwansecurity.org/TN/2004/TN-261104.htm.*
26. *http://taiwansecurity.org/TT/2004/TT-241104.htm.*

The Legislative Yuan election further heated up when Vice Premier Yeh Chu-lan called for voters to "terminate" those elements of the former GMD party-state when she lashed out at the injustices committed by the GMD in the 1950s. DPP government leaders kept up a relentless attack on the GMD coalition. It was on November 24th, according to Chin Heng-wei, editor-in-chief of *Contemporary Monthly*, that "GMD chairman Lien Chan challenged President Chen to have the DPP propose a referendum be held on the issue of unification or independence alongside the legislative polls." But, said Chin, "President Chen spiked the move with his reminder to Lien that it was the pan-blue camp who passed the so-called 'bird-cage' Referendum Law last November, which restricts the issues that the public can vote on in a referendum."[27]

On December 10th only 60 percent of registered voters cast their ballots, an all time low for such an important election. The DPP had been confident that its coalition could win a majority of the seats, but the DPP and TSU together only won 101 seats of the total 225, while the GMD-led coalition had won an unexpected victory because the historical trend of more voters supporting the DPP-led coalition ended.

Lien Chan interpreted the results as a victory for the GMD-led coalition. President Chen resigned his chairmanship of the DPP, took responsibility for his party's defeat, and said "lets turn our competition into a force for pushing the nation forward."[28] The U.S. government, which had repeatedly warned President Chen not to change the status quo, was relieved. The PRC regime spokespersons claimed the election result showed that most Tai-

27. *http://taiwansecurity.org/CNN/2004/CNN-111204.htm.*
28. *http://taiwansecurity.org/AFP/2004/AFP-151204.htm.*

wanese favor peace with the mainland and were disillusioned with the separatist activities of President Chen Shiubian.[29]

Cross-Taiwan Strait relations are now at a critical crossroads. Taiwan's two great political coalitions are highly factionalized and disagree about many things. For example, a large pro-Taiwan identity faction within the Guomindang led by Wang Jin-ping, President of the Legislative Yuan, along with former supporters of President Lee Teng-hui, want the GMD to maintain a low profile toward mainland China's authorities and to say nothing about re-unification of China. This "Taiwan identity faction" also has proposed policies similar to those of the DPP-led green coalition. A faction led by GMD chairman Lien Chan represents the moderate elements of the GMD Coalition who always wanted dialogue with the mainland authorities based on the 1992 "one China" principle consensus. A third faction, comprised of young GMD coalition members, appeals to all age groups to rally around the popular, charismatic Taipei mayor Ma Ying-jiou. Still reeling from its narrow presidential election defeat, the GMD-led blue coalition has not offered any clear vision for Taiwan's future, and how to check the expanding power of the DPP-led coalition.

But the DPP-led green coalition is also divided. The DPP has long been split into competing factions: one advocates compromise and forming a coalition with the GMD; another, more radical group advocates Taiwan independence and calls itself the "New Tide or *Xin Chao Liu*." The New Tide has always insisted upon confrontational struggle with the GMD to win elections. When the New Tide faction held its 20th anniversary on August 1, 2004, convener and lawmaker Tuan Yi-kang expressed his hope that the New Tide would improve relations with other party factions and thereby disband all factions to forge a strong DPP unity.[30]

29. *Taiwan Security Research* http://taiwansecurity.org/CP/2004/CP-070804 .htm.

30. *http://taiwansecurity.org/TN/2004/TN-020804.htm.*

Hong Chi-chang, a New Tide member and five other DPP law-makers also supported this proposal.

But at the DPP anniversary meeting in 2004, some break-throughs occurred in choosing a New Tide leader and forging DPP unity. Although the DPP always had factions, at the last minute of previous national elections of importance, compromise brought enough unity to win. By pursuing election-winning tactics for an incremental take-over of political power, the DPP now had taken control of both state and media. Not surprisingly, the DPP has steadily increased its electoral support from around 15 per-cent in the late 1980s to slightly over 50 percent in 2004.

But has Taiwan nationalism and separatism reached its lim-its? The December 2004 Legislative Yuan elections suggest that such a limit has been reached for the time being. Taiwan's voters are now equally divided. Roughly two-thirds of the voting popu-lace does not want to alter the "status quo" in Taiwan and pro-voke Beijing's leaders to use military force. The polity is divided along party lines, and the parties have competing factions. Voters are more cynical about Taiwan democracy and want consensus, so turnout is lower than in the past.

Prior to the March 2004 election, the PRC authorities had remained silent about political change in Taiwan, except when President Chen insisted upon attaching two referendums to that election and made certain claims while preparing for the Decem-ber 10, 2004, election. Washington and Beijing leaders persuaded Chen to water down his referendums until they were politically innocuous. After Chen's March 2004 election victory and his boasting that he wanted new referendums to reform the ROC Constitution, Beijing's authorities launched a concerted campaign to obtain American leadership support to discourage President Chen's tactics. Telephone calls between Beijing's top leaders and the White House increased and high visibility meetings by the

Taiwan Affairs Office of the State Council "stressed that the mainland aims to fight and contain separatist activities."

Wang Zaixi, vice-minister of the Taiwan affairs Office, put it this way: "So it is extremely dangerous for the Taiwan authorities to obstinately walk along the separatist road and mistakenly think the mainland will tolerate pro-independence activities for the benefit of its economic development and the 2008 Olympic Games."[31] Mainland China's academics, officials, and military personnel have warned Taiwan's authorities; U.S. government leaders, both in the executive and congressional branches of government, also have warned Taiwan. Their warnings should not be labeled a "barking dog" that does not bite, a phrase uttered by former President Lee Teng-hui in early 2004 when he tried to calm fears in Taiwan of Beijing's military threats. The tough rhetoric from the Beijing authorities also warned that military force would be used against Taiwan authorities if they crossed the "red line" to establish a Republic of Taiwan. For these reasons, an anti-secession law was promulgated in 2005 (see Appendix, document 7).

Meanwhile, in Taiwan new voices have begun speaking out against President Chen's championing of Taiwan independence. In August 2004, Hsu Hsin-liang, one of the fathers of Taiwan democracy and a former ally of President Chen, former chairman of the DPP, accused him of pushing the island to the brink of war with China. Hsu said that Chen's goal of adopting a new constitution by 2008 "was certain to bring disaster to the island because it will push China to invade. Chen Shui-bian's fundamentalist view on Taiwan independence will bring disaster. It's a foreseeable tragedy."[32] The 63 year-old political veteran also said he had already established a new political group to woo as many as 3

31. *China Daily* July 29, 2004, Vol. 24, No. 7160, p. 1.
32. *http://taiwansecurity.org/Reu/2004-040804-1.htm*.

million voters who worried about the DPP's policy toward China but were also frustrated by the GMD-led coalition's interest in overturning Chen's electoral victory. Hsu hoped to persuade more people to believe that a Taiwan-Mainland China, becoming integrated like the European Union, could ensure economic prosperity and peace in the region.

Further Readjustment of Beijing's Taiwan Policy

In early 2005, PRC leaders urged the ROC regime to renounce Taiwan nationalism and separatism. Jia Qinglin, Deputy Director of the CCP's Leading Group on Taiwan Affairs, stated that the PRC regime would talk to the DPP leaders about any topic if they renounced their "party's platform advocating Taiwan independence."[33] Wang Zaixi, Deputy Director of the Taiwan Affairs Office followed-up by informing the Taipei leadership that "Although the two sides are not yet reunited, the fact that both the mainland and Taiwan belong to one and the same China has never changed. That is the status quo of cross-strait relations."[34] Many interpreted this statement as a new version of the "One China" principle that ignored the sensitive issue of sovereignty, recognized the division of China, and also appealed to the Taiwan people.[35]

As PRC spokespersons adopted this friendly approach to the DPP leadership, on January 29, 2005 several mainland charter planes landed in Taiwan for the first time since 1949. A short time later Taiwan's charter planes landed in Beijing and Shanghai. These planes flew through Hong Kong airspace without the normal stopover, motivating Beijing to propose that more of the same charter flights continue.

33. *Renminribao*, Overseas Edition, January 25, 2005, p. 1.
34. *Renminribao*, Overseas Edition, January 25, 2005, p. 3.
35. *World Journal*, January 29, p. A1.

Just before President Chen was to meet with James Soong, PFP Chairman and critic of Taiwan independence, on February 24, 2005, President Chen gave his inauguration speech, saying that there was no major difference in the national identity of the ruling and opposition parties, or for that matter, the society itself, but that the President has the responsibility of defending the nation's sovereignty, security and dignity. Chairman Soong publicly warned the President that "self-deception cannot resolve confrontation, and we should begin by recognizing the ROC."[36] After both men met and talked, they issued a ten point joint declaration, stressing that "adherence to the ROC Constitution, preserving the status quo, and creating peace should be the supreme principles of today's cross-strait relations."

The Taiwan Solidarity Union (TSU) and Taiwan nationalists and separatists of the DPP condemned the Chen-Soong declaration, even calling for Chen to resign. But the general public welcomed the declaration and said it helped to calm cross-strait tensions. It was in this strange context—Beijing's urging Taipei's leaders to accept its solution to initiate the "three links" and the alliance between the DPP and PFP—that a new development occurred in Beijing that produced worldwide, mixed reactions toward the divided China struggle.

Beijing's Leaders Pass a New Law

PRC leaders knew very well that President Chen's administration was using all its resources to push the same policies—supporting Taiwan nationalism and separatism—that former President Lee had initiated, and that deeply worried them. How was it possible for the PRC regime to prevent the spiritual, psychological, and ideological transformation that the ROC regime was trying to

36. *World Journal*, February 24, p. A1.

impose upon its citizens, especially the young? How could the PRC regime stop creeping Taiwan nationalism and separatism? Had President Chen not set forth a timetable for Taiwan's independence, such as rewriting the ROC Constitution by 2006 and renaming the country as the Republic of Taiwan through referendum by 2008? Had Chen not changed the names of state enterprises to emphasize "Taiwan" instead of the "Republic of China" and inserted "Taiwan" into official correspondence from the ROC Foreign Ministry? PRC leaders now felt that without a law to restrain President Chen, he could take one step too many, producing a military conflict between the two sides.

PRC leaders now tried to establish rules that would be the equivalent of a law to discourage such behavior in Taiwan. They believed that such a law could eliminate shortcomings in PRC policy that the ROC regime could exploit to their advantage. They needed to have a law that made it impossible for those championing Taiwan independence to take advantage of ambiguities and uncertainties. The challenge for the PRC was to create a law that would permit the PRC to use force to restrain Taiwan from establishing or declaring independence from China, while providing sufficient incentives for the ROC regime to remain in the orbit of China. The law would be called "The Anti-Secession Law."

The reaction from the ROC regime and many parts of the world was critical of the new law. President Chen called on the PRC to abandon the law because it would make the distance across the Taiwan Strait greater. A U.S. State Department spokesman cautiously said the U.S. Government "does not think either side should take unilateral steps that try to define the situation further or push it in one direction or another."[37]

PRC leaders moved slowly and carefully to establish the new

---

37. Department of State Daily Briefing, Richard Boucher, Washington, D.C., February 15, 2005, at www.state.gov/r/pa/prs/dpb/2005.

law. President Hu Jintao stressed that his nation was eager for negotiations with the ROC regime. He urged President Chen to adhere to his inauguration promises to the people of Taiwan. President Hu also avoided any reference to "use of force" or "one country, two systems."[38]

Although many nations objected to the new law, the People's Congress passed the law on March 14, 2005. It contained ten articles with articles 1 and 3 reaffirming the "One China" principle, stating that both mainland and Taiwan make-up one China; the state shall not allow "Taiwan independence" secessionist forces to make Taiwan secede from China under any name or by any means. It emphasized that the divided China problem was a relic from China's civil war. Articles 4, 5, 6 articulated the conditions for peaceful unification and proposed measures to improve cross-strait relations. Article 7 called for negotiations between the two sides to discuss officially how to end hostility, determine Taiwan's political status, and consider international space for Taiwan.

Article 8 set forth the conditions that the state will use "non-peaceful means" to resolve the divided China problem. It specified that "In the event that the 'Taiwan independence' secessionist forces should act under any name or by any means to cause the fact of Taiwan's secession from China, or that major incidents entailing Taiwan's secession from China should occur, or that possibilities for a peaceful reunification should be completely exhausted, the state shall employ non-peaceful means and other necessary measures to protect China's sovereignty and territorial integrity." It also authorized the State Council and Central Military Commission to decide and execute the non-peaceful means, and then promptly report to the legislature.[39]

38. *World Journal*, March 5, p. A3.
39. *Renminribao*, online edition, www.english.people.com.cn/200503/14.

Reactions from the ROC regime came swiftly with 93 percent of respondents from an opinion survey saying they opposed the law that gave the PRC the right to use force against the Taiwan people.[40] More than half of the island's people believed the law mobilized popular support for President Chen's position on Taiwan independence.[41] President Chen said the law was an insult to Taiwan's democratic system. He urged the people to demonstrate on March 26 to oppose the law, and declared he would postpone his proposals for closer airline and commercial links. The U.S. State Department criticized the law as "unhelpful," saying it increased tensions, and Secretary Rice urged Beijing's leaders to offer conciliatory policies to improve an atmosphere now soured by the secession law.[42]

PRC officials insisted that the law merely restated existing Chinese law and policy. As one Taiwan scholar put it, "If we look at relations with China, nothing fundamental has changed."[43] Many scholars on both sides stated that the law simply tried to preserve the status quo and was intended not to change it. The law might serve as a watershed in future cross-strait relations. It made clear, by reference to legal statutes, the PRC's legal position regarding the divided China problem. In effect, the PRC regime established a red line for the ROC regime not to cross.

ROC Political Leaders Visit Mainland China

Disappointed by the DPP's failed efforts to improve Taiwan Strait relations, the GMD and PFP decided they would try to break the deadlock by organizing visits to the PRC to talk directly with Bei-

40. See *World Journal*, March 14, p. A3.
41. "Tide of Tension on Taiwan Strait," *Washington Post*, March 18, 2005, p. A14.
42. "China's Law on Taiwan Backfires," *Washington Post*, March 24, 2005, p. A13.
43. See *World Journal*, February 17, 2004, p. A2.

jing's leaders. In late March, Jiang Binkun, Vice Chairman of the GMD, returned from the mainland with an invitation from Hu Jintao to GMD Chairman Lien Chan to visit mainland China. Hu later invited James Soong to visit as well. Lien and Soong made their first visits in late April and early May respectively, the first time either had been in mainland China since World War II.

Hu and Lien met on April 29th in Beijing and agreed to uphold the "1992 Consensus," oppose Taiwan independence, and promote cross-strait relations. They issued a joint communiqué to achieve the goal of "a formal end to the state of hostility across the strait, agree to a peace treaty, and establish a framework for cross-strait peace and stability."[44]

Hu Jintao and James Soong met on May 11, and they too issued a joint declaration, agreeing that if Taiwan did not seek independence, there would not be any military conflict across the Taiwan Strait. It was the first time that Beijing used the term of "no independence, and no force (budu buwu)." This statement was praised by many in Taiwan as well as in the United States. Hu promised Soong that the PRC regime would expedite two-way direct flights across the strait by 2006, and exempt customs duties on Taiwan agricultural products as well as facilitating custom clearance of such products. Other promises were to speed-up the flow of people between the two sides, and to allow mainland Chinese tourists to visit Taiwan.[45]

The Hu-Soong declaration also contained an interesting proposal calling for both sides to embrace the principle of "two sides of the strait, one China" as a new framework to break the political stalemate and launch formal talks. Soong explained at a press conference that this new wording could provide a new ambiguity that allowed both sides to move beyond accusations and jump

---

44. *China Daily*, April 30, 2005, p. 1.
45. *China Daily*, May 12, p. 1 and May 13, 2005, p. 1.

start talks between the two sides. Soong said, "In fact, it is the 1992 consensus, but we are using 'two sides of the strait, one China,' so there is no need to debate past wording."[46] But President Chen immediately rejected this new proposal, saying that "China has not compromised at all; it offered nothing new."[47]

But a small majority of Taiwan's people supported these trips, and according to a Taipei opinion poll, 56 percent of Taiwan's people regarded Lien's trip as positive and conducive to developing peaceful cross-strait relations, while 51 percent praised his excellent performance. Another opinion poll by the *China Times* showed that more than half of the respondents welcomed the "no independence, no force" formula, and 40 percent endorsed Soong's trip to mainland China.[48] A new China fever spread throughout the island, and a political reassessment of cross-strait relations was under way.

46. "New Maxim From Beijing, 'Two sides of Strait,' is Met with a Yawn from Taiwan's President," *New York Times*, May 13, 2005, p. A8.

47. Ibid.

48. *World Journal*, April 30, 2005, p. A7.

7. Conclusion: Divided China's Continuing Struggle

"A healthy nation is as unconscious of its nationality as a healthy man of his bones. But if you break a nation's nationality it will think of nothing else but getting it set again."[1] When George Bernard Shaw uttered these words in 1904, little did he realize that he was describing the beliefs and sentiments of mainland China's and Taiwan's leaders and elites. In 1949, the Chinese Communist Party (CCP) had re-unified mainland China, except for the two colonies of Macao and Hong Kong, and the island of Taiwan and certain islands near mainland China, but in 2006 the reunification of Taiwan and mainland China still eluded China's leaders.

Mainland China's leaders and elites always have been obsessed with reunifying China, protecting its national security and territorial boundaries, and modernizing their nation to be an equal amongst the nations of the world. The GMD and CCP began their struggle to unify China in the early 1920s and continued until 1949, interrupted by Japanese imperialism and military aggression between 1937 and 1945. Mainland China's reunification came on October 1, 1949, and the ROC government moved to Taiwan, refusing to give up its dream of reunifying

1. John Gross, *The Oxford Book of Aphorisms* (Oxford and New York: Oxford University Press, 1983), p. 123.

China and modernizing it according to the doctrine of Sun Yat-sen.

During the 1950s, the PRC and ROC leaders believed they could achieve their goals, the primary being the reunification of China. Each regime believed its ideology and modernization strategies would enable it to prevail over the other. The historical burden of China's reunification fell heavily upon PRC's leaders, Mao and others, who committed their careers and prestige to completing their historical mission. The GMD's leaders, Chiang Kai-shek and Chiang Ching-kuo, pursued this historical mission. After Chiang Ching-kuo died in 1988, the DPP challenged the GMD leadership and, in 2000, that party replaced the GMD and a new era of political struggle in Taiwan began.

In mainland China, the PRC's leaders still clung to their dream of China's reunification. Their strong nationalist sentiments galvanized them to block any Chinese territory that tried to secede from China stipulated in the PRC Constitution. As for Taiwan's new leaders, who believed in Taiwan nationalism and separatism, the PRC's leaders have repeatedly warned they will use force, if necessary, to reunify China. Their reasons are the following.

First, Taiwan will always be a lightning rod reminding Beijing's leaders that the U.S. Government intervened in China's civil war and prevented them from resolving the divided China problem on Beijing's terms. Second, CCP leaders believe that if Taiwan separates from mainland China, they will have lost their legitimacy to govern. Third, Taiwan is strategically important to mainland China. Finally, the People's Liberation Army has promised the people it will bring Taiwan to heel if ordered to do so, and any failure to do that would produce a legitimacy crisis for the government.[2]

2. The Jamestown Foundation, "Why Taiwan Really Matters to China,"

Twice, the United States, for unexpected foreign policy reasons, intervened in the Chinese civil war. In June 1950, President Harry Truman dispatched naval forces to the Taiwan Strait to prevent war between the two sides. In early 1979 Congress passed the Taiwan Relations Act, mandating the U.S. government to supply weapons to Taiwan and use force, if necessary, to ensure a peaceful negotiation of the divided China problem.

The U.S. government justified these interventions in the pursuit of America's national interests. The U.S. did not want another war in the Taiwan Strait, and its leaders hoped that eventually these opposing Chinese regimes might peacefully resolve their differences. In the second instance, the U.S. hoped to cooperate with the PRC to counter the expanding military power of the Soviet Union. To achieve its diverse national interests the U.S. had readjusted its Taiwan policy accordingly.

Between 1991 and 2006, public opinion and voting behavior in Taiwan began to change. Instead of supporting China's reunification, as in the past, more voters began to embrace a new national identity, Taiwan nationalism. They strongly believed that democracy gave them the right for self-determination: to use a public referendum to build a Republic of Taiwan. Opinion polls revealed that a growing proportion of voters were expressing their national identity as being Taiwanese and not Taiwanese and Chinese as in the past. The national elections held in 2004 for the presidency and the parliament clearly showed a society equally divided in their political preferences for the DPP or the GMD.

A new group of voters also emerged. According to many opinion polls, they make-up roughly 55 to 65 percent of all voters who do not want Taiwan's political system to be radically changed by referendums and elections. This group prefers maintaining the

China Brief, 4:19 (September 30, 2004) and *http://pubs@jamestown.org/ publications_id=395&issue=id=3090&article_id=2368616.*

status quo of current public opinion. That is to say, they want to avoid extreme political outcomes like rapid independence from mainland China or rapid reunification with mainland China. This group wants improved government performance, less corruption, better economic relations with the PRC regime, and Taiwan's participation in international organizations, as well as having diplomatic relations with other nations.

From 1999 until 2006 the two regimes have not held direct talks. Two types of disagreement characterize Taiwan society and the divided China problem. The first disagreement is between the Taiwan and mainland China governments as to how they can negotiate the termination of the civil war and how to normalize relations to resolve the divided China problem. The reason for the lack of dialogue is that the DPP government does not agree that Taiwan is part of China, although the ROC's Constitution stipulates just that. The DPP leaders insist that dialogue resume, on the condition that two independent, sovereign states exist on both sides of the Taiwan Strait.

The second type of disagreement is between Taiwan's GMD-led coalition and the DPP-led coalition. They refuse to cooperate with each other, because they are unwilling to agree on the principles for how representatives of the ROC and PRC regimes can negotiate to resolve their differences. Moreover, they disagree on many issues advanced by their respective legislators in the parliament. Thus political gridlock paralyzes the government.

There is also enormous confusion, not just amongst voters in Taiwan, but in capitals around the world, as to why these two types of disagreements have come about.

From 1979 until around 2002, the PRC policy toward Taiwan and other nations was based upon agreeing to an acceptable standard to define Taiwan's status in the world of nation states. The PRC leaders agreed to define that standard in terms of a "One China Principle." That is to say, Taiwan is, and always has been, part of China, whose capital is Beijing and is now represented by the PRC government and its Constitution. All nations desiring diplomatic relations with the PRC had to agree to this "One China Principle" if they wanted to establish diplomatic ties with the PRC. For this reason, less than 30 states now formally recognize the ROC as a sovereign state, but more than 150 nations do not recognize the ROC as a sovereign state. In addition to establishing the standard called the "One China Principle" the PRC government also proposed to the ROC regime that reunification be based upon the "one country, two system" principle. Under this principle, the ROC regime would have a high degree of autonomy, and the first stage of China's reunification could begin.

These two principles signified a specific diplomatic track that the PRC regime had adopted to conclude the Chinese civil war and begin the reunification of China. But both Taiwan's Presidents Lee and Chen refused to agree to these principles and rejected the PRC's foreign policy track for negotiations. After the DPP won the 2000 March presidential election, the PRC leaders began to re-think their "One China Principle."

They were motivated to do so because PRC leaders now realized that Taiwan's citizens had few reasons to admire and trust the PRC and its modernization path. They also worried that when the DPP government promoted Taiwan nationalism and separatism, fewer people would favor strengthening their roots with Chinese civilization, culture, and Confucian ideology. They knew that President Chen had no intention of accepting the 1992 Consensus, and he repeatedly rejected the "One China Principle" as any basis for beginning a dialogue with Beijing's leaders. In fact, whenever President Chen proposed that Taiwan be admitted into WHO or the United Nations, and the PRC mobilized international support to oppose such admission, President Chen could then inform Taiwan's people that the PRC did not care about them. In this way many Taiwanese deeply resented the PRC and its policies toward Taiwan.

The PRC leaders realized that the only way these trends could be checked, and even reversed, was to integrate the market economies of Taiwan and mainland China and to promote greater exchange of peoples for integrating their societies as well. For these reasons the PRC regime tried to conceptualize a new "One China Principle" that would be acceptable to both sides to jump start negotiations. In this way, Beijing's leaders hoped to persuade the Taiwan people that their future lay with allying closely with mainland China's people.

Thus, the PRC proposed a new "One China" principle that boils down to be the following: Taiwan and mainland China make up China and the sovereignty of "One China" cannot be divided. Under this principle all issues can be discussed by equal partners. But the Chen administration never responded to this new "One China" principle. Nor has this principle been debated in Taiwan. Meanwhile, two different "One China Principles" now exist, and that is the reason for much misunderstanding and confusion, not only within Taiwan, but worldwide as well.[3]

Given the two types of disagreements that have polarized Taiwan's society, and created the confusion over two different "One China Principles," can the divided China problem be peacefully resolved?

It is too early to determine if Taiwan's current equilibrium, its political balance of power, will hold for very long. Much depends upon how voters succeed in balancing the political forces, so that debate and dialogue can resolve the two fundamental types of disagreements described above. Taiwan's voters must think deeply about the issues, vote for capable leaders, and not simply

3. The late Wang Daohan explained this problem to the authors when they visited him in Shanghai, just before the fiftieth anniversary of the birth of the PRC.

vote according to party loyalty. Therefore, Taiwan voters need more time to improve the performance of their democracy, and to allow mainland China's leaders more time to modernize in ways familiar to, and compatible with the experiences of Taiwan's people.

One rule of thumb voters and politicians might adopt is to utilize Taiwan's democracy and productive market economy to influence positive change in mainland China. Taiwan's political leaders, elites, and voters have not thought deeply about how to take advantage of their power.

The more successful mainland China's leaders are in modernizing China, in ways familiar to Taiwan's people, the more inclined Taiwan's people will be to improve their society and participate in China's modernization. If mainland China's leaders fail in their modernization, there will be no incentives for Taiwan's people to seek China's reunification. Other territories such as Tibet, Macao, and Hong Kong, along with other provinces, will have every incentive to demand greater autonomy and even independence.

Modernization and reunification are long-term processes. Much unanticipated change is bound to occur across the Taiwan Strait in the near future and beyond, some good and some bad. Such change will produce optimism or despair about future trends. However these trends unfold, the ROC regime has the resiliency and ability to survive in today's world. Taiwan's history also confirms this. Thus, ROC leaders must be pragmatic and realize that although different states, independent and sovereign, exist across the Taiwan Strait, Chinese history and civilization also have evolved on both sides of the Taiwan Strait. Why should they try to obliterate that history and destroy those forces of today that are trying to preserve that history?

Is it not true that the advantages of joining together to work toward a "One China" far outweigh the disadvantages? The ROC regime has a privileged position of watching and participating in the experimental transformation of mainland China into a new society and polity. These moral and national security reasons alone justify that mainland and Taiwan sit down as equals, to discuss how they can co-exist and work as partners in the building of a new Chinese civilization with the cultural and ethnic pluralism that exists in so many societies today.

With wisdom, patience, tolerance, and understanding, each regime should be able to find ways to assist the other and avoid imposing selfish demands upon the other. For these reasons, there should be healthy debate in Taiwan so that people can ruminate about the new proposals by the PRC leaders. If opposed, Taiwan's elites can clearly explain their opposition. Mainland China elites should also participate in this debate. Only in this way can the peoples on both sides of the Taiwan Strait understand their mutual fears and aspirations and make these important building blocks for nurturing trust.

Taiwan holds a trump card to be played. Its elites can mobilize citizens of the island to engage the mainland in earnest, sincere negotiations for a "One Country Two System" of a federation or commonwealth political system. Political party leaders, elites and ordinary people should ponder the new "One China Principle" that Beijing has offered Taipei. Ultimately, Taiwan's people might reassess their options and experiment for a reasonable period in cautious cooperation with their mainland China counterparts.

Before the 2008 presidential election, it is still possible for the GMD-led coalition to work with status quo voters, especially those favoring the DPP. Creative political leadership, making reference to the 1948 Constitution, could argue the point that a "One China" with different societies and polities is the ultimate challenge for building trust and exploring how cooperation can be leveraged to remove fear and distrust. If enough DPP members and independents support this approach, they should be able to elicit support from the PRC side to expand Taiwan's "international space" and to consider the federation or commonwealth polity as an arrangement to overcome the past. Gradually, the divided China struggle would be moderated and relegated to the past.

Appendix:
Key Documents

1. The Joint U.S.-China Communiqué,
   Shanghai, February 27, 1972

2. Joint Communiqué on Establishment of U.S.-PRC
   Diplomatic Relations, January 1, 1979

3. Taiwan Relations Act, April 10, 1979

4. U.S.-PRC Joint Communiqué, August 17, 1982

5. Guidelines for National Unification, February 23, 1991

6. Continue to Promote the Reunification of China
   (The Eight-Point Policy by Jiang Zemin),
   January 30, 1995

7. Anti-Secession Law, March 2005

1. The Joint U.S.-China Communiqué, Shanghai, February 27, 1972

President Richard Nixon of the United States of America visited the People's Republic of China at the invitation of Premier Chou En-lai of the People's Republic of China from February 21 to February 28, 1972. Accompanying the President were Mrs. Nixon, U.S. Secretary of State William Rogers, Assistant to the President Dr. Henry Kissinger, and other American officials.

President Nixon met with Chairman Mao Tse-tung of the Communist Party of China on February 21. The two leaders had a serious and frank exchange of views on Sino-U.S. relations and world affairs.

During the visit, extensive, earnest and frank discussions were held between President Nixon and Premier Chou En-lai on the normalization of relations between the United States of America and the People's Republic of China, as well as on other matters of interest to both sides. In addition, Secretary of State William Rogers and Foreign Minister Chi Peng-fei held talks in the same spirit.

President Nixon and his party visited Peking and viewed cultural, industrial and agricultural sites, and they also toured Hangchow and Shanghai where, continuing discussions with Chinese leaders, they viewed similar places of interest.

The leaders of the People's Republic of China and the United States of America found it beneficial to have this opportunity, after so many years without contact, to present candidly to one another their views on a variety of issues. They reviewed the international situation in which important changes and great upheavals are taking place and expounded their respective positions and attitudes.

The U.S. side stated: Peace in Asia and peace in the world requires efforts both to reduce immediate tensions and to eliminate the basic causes of conflict. The United States will work for a just and secure peace: just, because it fulfills the aspirations of peoples and nations for freedom and progress; secure, because it removes the danger of foreign aggression. The United States supports individual freedom and social progress for all the peoples of the world, free of outside pressure or intervention. The United States believes that the effort to reduce tensions is served by improving communication between countries that through accident, miscalculation or misunderstanding. Countries should treat each other with mutual respect and be willing to compete peacefully, letting performance be the ultimate judge. No country should claim infallibility and each country should be pre-pared to re-examine its own attitudes for the common good. The United States stressed that: the peoples of Indochina should be allowed to determine their destiny without outside intervention; its constant primary objective has been a negotiated solution; the eight-point proposal put forward by the Republic of Vietnam and the United States on January 27, 1972 represents a basis for the attain-ment of that objective; in the absence of a negotiated settlement the United States envisages the ultimate withdrawal of all U.S. forces from the region consistent with the aim of self-determination for each country of Indochina. The United States will maintain its close ties with and support for the Republic of Korea; the United States will support efforts of the Republic of Korea to seek a relaxation of tension and increased communication in the Korean peninsula. The United States places the highest value on its friendly relations with Japan; it will continue to develop the existing close bonds. Consistent with the United Nations Security Council Resolution of December 21, 1971, the United States favors the continuation of the ceasefire between India and Pakistan and the withdrawal of all military forces to within their own territories and to their own sides of the ceasefire line in Jammu and Kashmir; the United States supports the right of the peo-ples of South Asia to shape their own future in peace, free of military threat, and without having the area become the subject of great power rivalry.

The Chinese side stated: Wherever there is oppression, there is resistance. Countries want independence, nations want liberation and the people want revolution—this has become the irresistible trend of history. All nations, big or small, should be equal; big nations should not bully the small and strong nations should not bully the weak. China will never be a superpower and it opposes hegemony and power politics of any kind. The Chinese side stated that it firmly supports the struggles of all the oppressed people and nations for freedom and liberation and that the people of all countries have the right to choose their social systems according to their own wishes and the right to safeguard the independence, sovereignty and territorial integrity of their own countries and oppose foreign aggression, interference, control and subversion. All foreign troops should be withdrawn to their own countries.

The Chinese side expressed its firm support to the peoples of Vietnam, Laos and Cambodia in their efforts for the attainment of their goal and its firm support to the seven-point proposal of the Provisional Revolutionary Government of the Republic of South Vietnam and the elaboration of February this year on the two key problems in the proposal, and to the Joint Declaration of the Summit Conference of the Indochinese Peoples. It firmly supports the eight-point program for the peaceful unification of Korea put forward by the Government of the Democratic People's Republic of Korea on April 12, 1971, and the stand for the abolition of the "U.N. Commission for the Unification and Rehabilitation of Korea." It firmly opposes the revival and outward expansion of Japanese militarism and firmly supports the Japanese people's desire to build an independent, democratic, peaceful and neutral Japan. It firmly maintains that India and Pakistan should, in accordance with the United Nations resolutions on the India-Pakistan question, immediately withdraw all their forces to their respective territories and to their own sides of the ceasefire line in Jammu and Kashmir and firmly supports the Pakistan Government and people in their struggle to preserve their independence and sovereignty and the people of Jammu and Kashmir in their struggle for the right of self-determination.

There are essential differences between China and the United States in their social systems and foreign policies. However, the two sides agreed that countries, regardless of their social systems, should conduct their relations on the principles of respect for the sovereignty and territorial integrity of all states, non-aggression against other states, non-interference in the internal affairs of other states, equality and mutual benefit, and peaceful coexistence. International disputes should be settled on this basis, without resorting to the use or threat of force. The United States and the People's Republic of China are prepared to apply these principles to their mutual relations.

With these principles of international relations in mind the two sides stated that:

- progress toward the normalization of relations between China and the United States is in the interests of all countries;

- both wish to reduce the danger of international military conflict;

- neither should seek hegemony in the Asia-Pacific region and each is opposed to efforts by any other country or group of countries to establish such hegemony; and

- neither is prepared to negotiate on behalf of any third party or to enter into agreements or understandings with the other directed at other states.

Both sides are of the view that it would be against the interests of the peoples of the world for any major country to collude with another against other countries, or for major countries to divide up the world into spheres of interest.

The two sides reviewed the long-standing serious disputes between China and the United States. The Chinese side reaffirmed its position: The Taiwan question is the crucial question obstructing the normalization of relations between China and the United States; the Government of the People's Republic of China is the sole legal government of China; Taiwan is a province of China which has long been returned to the motherland; the liberation of Taiwan is China's internal affair in which no other country has the right to interfere; and all U.S. forces and military installations must be withdrawn from Taiwan. The Chinese Government firmly opposes any activities which aim at the creation of "one China, one Taiwan," "one China, two governments," "two Chinas," and "independent Taiwan" or advocate that "the status of Taiwan remains to be determined."

The U.S. side declared: The United States acknowledges that all Chinese on either side of the Taiwan Strait maintain there is but one China and that Taiwan is a part of China. The United States Government does not challenge that position. It reaffirms its interest in a peaceful settlement of the Taiwan question by the Chinese themselves. With this prospect in mind, it affirms the ultimate objective of the withdrawal of all U.S. forces and military installations from Taiwan. In the meantime, it will progressively reduce its forces and military installations on Taiwan as the tension in the area diminishes.

The two sides agreed that it is desirable to broaden the understanding between the two peoples. To this end, they discussed specific areas in such fields as science, technology, culture, sports and journalism, in which people-to-people contacts and exchanges would be mutually beneficial. Each side undertakes to facilitate the further development of such contacts and exchanges.

Both sides view bilateral trade as another area from which mutual benefit can be derived, and agreed that economic relations based on equality and mutual benefit are in the interest of the peoples of the two countries. They agree to facilitate the progressive development of trade between their two countries.

The two sides agreed that they will stay in contact through various channels, including the sending of a senior U.S. representative to Peking from time to time for concrete consultations to further the normalization of relations between the two countries and continue to exchange views on issues of common interest.

The two sides expressed the hope that the gains achieved during this visit would open up new prospects for the relations between the two countries. They believe that the normalization of relations between the two countries is not only in the interest of the Chinese and American peoples but also contributes to the relaxation of tension in Asia and the world.

President Nixon, Mrs. Nixon and the American party expressed their appreciation for the gracious hospitality shown them by the Government and people of the People's Republic of China.

2. Joint Communiqué on Establishment of U.S.-PRC Diplomatic Relations, January 1, 1979

(The communiqué was released on December 15, 1978, in Washington and Peking.)

The United States of America and the People's Republic of China have agreed to recognize each other and to establish diplomatic relations as of January 1, 1979.

The United States of America recognizes the Government of the People's Republic of China as the sole legal Government of China. Within this context, the people of the United States will maintain cultural, commercial, and other unofficial relations with the people of Taiwan.

The United States of America and the People's Republic of China reaffirm the principles agreed on by the two sides in the Shanghai Communiqué and emphasize once again that:

- Both wish to reduce the danger of international military conflict.

- Neither should seek hegemony in the Asia-Pacific region or in any other region of the world and each is opposed to efforts by any other country or group of countries to establish such hegemony.

- Neither is prepared to negotiate on behalf of any third party or to enter into agreements or understandings with the other directed at other states.

- The Government of the United States of America acknowledges the Chinese position that there is but one China and Taiwan is part of China.

- Both believe that normalization of Sino-American relations is not only in the interest of the Chinese and American peoples but also contributes to the cause of peace in Asia and the world.

The United States of America and the People's Republic of China will exchange Ambassadors and establish Embassies on March 1, 1979.

3. Taiwan Relations Act, April 10, 1979

Note: Several revisions were made to Public Law 96-8 when it was codified. Sections 1 and 18 of the Public Law were omitted, as was Section 12(d). In addition, the United States Code contains a section not included in the original Act, Section 3310a. The United States Code version is the authoritative version of the Act.

An Act

To help maintain peace, security, and stability in the Western Pacific and to promote the foreign policy of the United States by authorizing the continuation of commercial, cultural, and other relations between the people of the United States and the people on Taiwan, and for other purposes.

Be it enacted by the Senate and House of Representatives of the United States of America in Congress assembled,

- SHORT TITLE
  - SECTION 1. This Act may be cited as the "Taiwan Relations Act".

- FINDINGS AND DECLARATION OF POLICY
  - SEC. 2. (a) The President—having terminated governmental relations between the United States and the governing authorities on Taiwan recognized by the United States as the Republic of China prior to January 1, 1979, the Congress finds that the enactment of this Act is necessary—
    - (1) to help maintain peace, security, and stability in the Western Pacific; and

- (2) to promote the foreign policy of the United States by authorizing the continuation of commercial, cultural, and other relations between the people of the United States and the people on Taiwan.
- (b) It is the policy of the United States—
  - (1) to preserve and promote extensive, close, and friendly commercial, cultural, and other relations between the people of the United States and the people on Taiwan, as well as the people on the China mainland and all other peoples of the Western Pacific area;
  - (2) to declare that peace and stability in the area are in the political, security, and economic interests of the United States, and are matters of international concern;
  - (3) to make clear that the United States decision to establish diplomatic relations with the People's Republic of China rests upon the expectation that the future of Taiwan will be determined by peaceful means;
  - (4) to consider any effort to determine the future of Taiwan by other than peaceful means, including by boycotts or embargoes, a threat to the peace and security of the Western Pacific area and of grave concern to the United States;
  - (5) to provide Taiwan with arms of a defensive character; and
  - (6) to maintain the capacity of the United States to resist any resort to force or other forms of coercion that would jeopardize the security, or the social or economic system, of the people on Taiwan.
- (c) Human rights—Nothing contained in this chapter shall contravene the interest of the United States in human rights, especially with respect to the human rights of all the approximately eighteen million inhabitants of Taiwan. The preservation and enhancement of the human rights of all the people on Taiwan are hereby reaffirmed as objectives of the United States.

- IMPLEMENTATION OF UNITED STATES POLICY WITH REGARD TO TAIWAN
    - SEC. 3. (a) In furtherance of the policy set forth in section 2 of this Act, the United States will make available to Taiwan such defense articles and defense services in such quantity as may be necessary to enable Taiwan to maintain a sufficient self-defense capability.
    - (b) The President and the Congress shall determine the nature and quantity of such defense articles and services based solely upon their judgment of the needs of Taiwan, in accordance with procedures established by law. Such determination of Taiwan's defense needs shall include review by United States military authorities in connection with recommendations to the President and the Congress.
    - (c) The President is directed to inform the Congress promptly of any threat to the security or the social or economic system of the people on Taiwan and any danger to the interests of the United States arising therefrom. The President and the Congress shall determine, in accordance with constitutional processes, appropriate action by the United States in response to any such danger.

- APPLICATION OF LAWS; INTERNATIONAL AGREEMENTS
    - SEC. 4. (a) The absence of diplomatic relations or recognition shall not affect the application of the laws of the United States with respect to Taiwan, and the laws of the United States shall apply with respect to Taiwan in the manner that the laws of the United States applied with respect to Taiwan prior to January 1, 1979.
    - (b) The application of subsection (a) of this section shall include, but shall not be limited to, the following:
        - (1) Whenever the laws of the United States refer or relate to foreign countries, nations, states, governments, or similar entities, such terms shall include and such laws shall apply with respect to Taiwan.
        - (2) Whenever authorized by or pursuant to the laws of the United States to conduct or carry out programs, transactions, or other relations with respect to

foreign countries, nations, states, governments, or similar entities, the President or any agency of the United States Government is authorized to conduct and carry out, in accordance with section 6 of this Act, such programs, transactions, and other relations with respect to Taiwan (including, but not limited to, the performance of services for the United States through contracts with commercial entities on Taiwan), in accordance with the applicable laws of the United States.

- (3)(A) The absence of diplomatic relations and recognition with respect to Taiwan shall not abrogate, infringe, modify, deny, or otherwise affect in any way any rights or obligations (including but not limited to those involving contracts, debts, or property interests of any kind) under the laws of the United States heretofore or hereafter acquired by or with respect to Taiwan.

- (B) For all purposes under the laws of the United States, including actions in any court in the United States, recognition of the People's Republic of China shall not affect in any way the ownership of or other rights or interests in properties, tangible and intangible, and other things of value, owned or held on or prior to December 31, 1978, or thereafter acquired or earned by the governing authorities on Taiwan.

- (4) Whenever the application of the laws of the United States depends upon the law that is or was applicable on Taiwan or compliance therewith, the law applied by the people on Taiwan shall be considered the applicable law for that purpose.

- (5) Nothing in this Act, nor the facts of the President's action in extending diplomatic recognition to the People's Republic of China, the absence of diplomatic relations between the people on Taiwan and the United States, or the lack of recognition by the United States, and attendant circumstances thereto, shall be construed in any administrative or judicial proceeding as a basis for any United States Government agency, commission, or department to make a finding of fact or determination of law, under the Atomic Energy Act of 1954 and the Nuclear Non-Proliferation Act of 1978, to deny an export license application or to revoke an existing export license for nuclear exports to Taiwan.

- (6) For purposes of the Immigration and Nationality Act, Taiwan may be treated in the manner specified in the first sentence of section 202(b) of that Act.
- (7) The capacity of Taiwan to sue and be sued in courts in the United States, in accordance with the laws of the United States, shall not be abrogated, infringed, modified, denied, or otherwise affected in any way by the absence of diplomatic relations or recognition.
- (8) No requirement, whether expressed or implied, under the laws of the United States with respect to maintenance of diplomatic relations or recognition shall be applicable with respect to Taiwan.

  - (c) For all purposes, including actions in any court in the United States, the Congress approves the continuation in force of all treaties and other international agreements, including multilateral conventions, entered into by the United States and the governing authorities on Taiwan recognized by the United States as the Republic of China prior to January 1, 1979, and in force between them on December 31, 1978, unless and until terminated in accordance with law.
  - (d) Nothing in this Act may be construed as a basis for supporting the exclusion or expulsion of Taiwan from continued membership in any international financial institution or any other international organization.

- OVERSEAS PRIVATE INVESTMENT CORPORATION
  - SEC. 5. (a) During the three-year period beginning on the date of enactment of this Act, the $1,000 per capita income restriction in insurance, clause (2) of the second

undesignated paragraph of section 231 of the reinsurance, Foreign Assistance Act of 1961 shall not restrict the activities of the Overseas Private Investment Corporation in determining whether to provide any insurance, reinsurance, loans, or guaranties with respect to investment projects on Taiwan.

○ (b) Except as provided in subsection (a) of this section, in issuing insurance, reinsurance, loans, or guaranties with respect to investment projects on Taiwan, the Overseas Private Insurance
[1] Corporation shall apply the same criteria as those applicable in other parts of the world. *[1] Note: So in original. Probably should be "Investment".*

- THE AMERICAN INSTITUTE OF TAIWAN
  ○ SEC. 6. (a) Programs, transactions, and other relations conducted or carried out by the President or any agency of the United States Government with respect to Taiwan shall, in the manner and to the extent directed by the President, be conducted and carried out by or through—
    - (1) The American Institute in Taiwan, a nonprofit corporation incorporated under the laws of the District of Columbia, or
    - (2) such comparable successor nongovermental entity as the President may designate, (hereafter in this Act referred to as the "Institute").
  ○ (b) Whenever the President or any agency of the United States Government is authorized or required by or pursuant to the laws of the United States to enter into, perform, enforce, or have in force an agreement or transaction relative to Taiwan, such agreement or transaction shall be entered into, performed, and enforced, in the manner and to the extent directed by the President, by or through the Institute.
  ○ (c) To the extent that any law, rule, regulation, or ordinance of the District of Columbia, or of any State or political subdivision thereof in which the Institute is incorporated or doing business, impedes or otherwise

interferes with the performance of the functions of the Institute pursuant to this Act; such law, rule, regulation, or ordinance shall be deemed to be preempted by this Act.

- SERVICES BY THE INSTITUTE TO UNITED STATES CITIZENS ON TAIWAN
  - SEC. 7. (a) The Institute may authorize any of its employees on Taiwan—
    - (1) to administer to or take from any person an oath, affirmation, affidavit, or deposition, and to perform any notarial act which any notary public is required or authorized by law to perform within the United States;
    - (2) To [1] act as provisional conservator of the personal estates of deceased United States citizens; and
      [1] Note: *So in original. Probably should not be capitalized.*
    - (3) to assist and protect the interests of United States persons by performing other acts such as are authorized to be performed outside the United States for consular purposes by such laws of the United States as the President may specify.
  - (b) Acts performed by authorized employees of the Institute under this section shall be valid, and of like force and effect within the United States, as if performed by any other person authorized under the laws of the United States to perform such acts.

- TAX EXEMPT STATUS OF THE INSTITUTE
  - SEC. 8. (a) The Institute, its property, and its income are exempt from all taxation now or hereafter imposed by the United States (except to the extent that section 11(a)(3) of this Act requires the imposition of taxes imposed under chapter 21 of the Internal Revenue Code of 1954, relating to the Federal Insurance Contributions Act) or by State or local taxing authority of the United States.
  - (b) For purposes of the Internal Revenue Code of 1954, the Institute shall be treated as an organization described

in sections 170(b)(1)(A), 170(c), 2055(a), 2106(a)(2)(A),, 2522(a), and 2522(b).

- FURNISHING PROPERTY AND SERVICES TO AND OBTAIN-ING SERVICES FROM THE INSTITUTE
  - SEC. 9. (a) Any agency of the United States Government is authorized to sell, loan, or lease property (including interests therein) to, and to perform administrative and technical support functions and services for the operations of, the Institute upon such terms and conditions as the President may direct. Reimbursements to agencies under this subsection shall be credited to the current applicable appropriation of the agency concerned.
  - (b) Any agency of the United States Government is authorized to acquire and accept services from the Institute upon such terms and conditions as the President may direct. Whenever the President determines it to be in furtherance of the purposes of this Act, the procurement of services by such agencies from the Institute may be effected without regard to such laws of the United States normally applicable to the acquisition of services by such agencies as the President may specify by Executive order.
  - (c) Any agency of the United States Government making funds available to the Institute in accordance with this Act shall make arrangements with the Institute for the Comptroller General of the United States to have access to the; books and records of the Institute and the opportunity to audit the operations of the Institute.

- TAIWAN INSTRUMENTALITY
  - SEC. 10. (a) Whenever the President or any agency of the United States Government is authorized or required by or pursuant to the laws of the United States to render or provide to or to receive or accept from Taiwan, any performance, communication, assurance, undertaking, or other action, such action shall, in the manner and to the. extent directed by the President, be rendered or Provided to, or received or accepted from, an instrumentality established by Taiwan which the President determines has the

necessary authority under the laws applied by the people on Taiwan to provide assurances and take other actions on behalf of Taiwan in accordance with this Act.

○ (b) The President is requested to extend to the instrumentality established by Taiwan the same number of offices and complement of personnel as were previously operated in the United States by the governing authorities on Taiwan recognized as the Republic of China prior to January 1, 1979.

○ (c) Upon the granting by Taiwan of comparable privileges and immunities with respect to the Institute and its appropriate personnel, the President is authorized to extend with respect to the Taiwan instrumentality and its appropriate; personnel, such privileges and immunities (subject to appropriate conditions and obligations) as may be necessary for the effective performance of their functions.

- SEPARATION OF GOVERNMENT PERSONNEL FOR EMPLOYMENT WITH THE INSTITUTE

  ○ SEC. 11. (a)(1) Under such terms and conditions as the President may direct, any agency of the United States Government may separate from Government service for a specified period any officer or employee of that agency who accepts employment with the Institute.

  ○ (2) An officer or employee separated by an agency under paragraph (1) of this subsection for employment with the Institute shall be entitled upon termination of such employment to reemployment or reinstatement with such agency (or a successor agency) in an appropriate position with the attendant rights, privileges, and benefits with [1] the officer or employee would have had or acquired had he or she not been so separated, subject to such time period and other conditions as the President may prescribe.

  [1] Note: So in original. Probably should be "which".

  ○ (3) An officer or employee entitled to reemployment or reinstatement rights under paragraph (2) of this subsection shall, while continuously employed by the Institute with no break in continuity of service, continue to participate in any benefit program in which such officer or employee was participating prior to employment by the Institute, including programs for compensation for job-related death, injury, or illness; programs for health and life insurance; programs for annual, sick, and other statutory leave; and programs for retirement under any system established by the laws of the United States; except that employment with the Institute shall be the basis for participation in such programs only to the extent that employee deductions and employer contributions, as required, in payment for such participation for the period of employment with the Institute, are currently deposited in the program's or system's fund or depository. Death or retirement of any such officer or employee during approved service with the Institute and prior to reemployment or reinstatement shall be considered a death in or retirement from Government service for purposes of any employee or survivor benefits acquired by reason of service with an agency of the United States Government.

○ (4) Any officer or employee of an agency of the United States Government who entered into service with the Institute on approved leave of absence without pay prior to the enactment of this Act shall receive the benefits of this section for the period of such service.

○ (b) Any agency of the United States Government employing alien personnel on Taiwan may transfer such personnel, with accrued allowances, benefits, and rights, to the Institute without a break in service for purposes of retirement and other benefits, including continued participation in any system established by the laws of the United States for the retirement of employees in which the alien was participating prior to the transfer to the Institute, except that employment with the Institute shall be creditable for retirement purposes only to the extent that employee deductions and employer contributions as required, in payment for such participation for the period of employment with the Institute, are currently deposited in the system's fund or depository.

○ (c) Employees of the Institute shall not be employees of the United States and, in representing the Institute, shall be exempt from section 207 of title 18, United States Code.

○ (d)(1) For purposes of sections 911 and 913 of the Internal Revenue Code of 1954, amounts paid by the Institute to its employees shall not be treated as earned income. Amounts received by employees of the Institute shall not be:included in gross income, and shall be exempt from taxation, to the extent that they are equivalent to amounts received by civilian officers and employees of the Government of the United States as allowances and benefits which are exempt from taxation under section 912 of such Code.

○ (2) Except to the extent required by subsection (a)(3) of this section, service performed in the employ of the Institute shall not constitute employment for purposes of chapter 21 of such Code and title II of the Social Security Act.

● REPORTING REQUIREMENT
    ○ SEC. 12. (a) The Secretary of State shall transmit to the Congress the text of any agreement to which the Institute is a party. However, any such agreement the immediate public disclosure of which would, in the opinion of the President, be prejudicial to the national security of the United States shall not be so transmitted to the Congress but shall be transmitted to the Committee on Foreign Relations of the Senate and the Committee on Foreign Affairs of the House of Representatives under an appropriate injunction of secrecy to be removed only upon due notice from the President.
    ○ (b) For purposes of subsection (a), the term "agreement" includes—
        ▪ (1) any agreement entered into between the Institute and the governing authorities on Taiwan or the instrumentality established by Taiwan; and

- (2) any agreement entered into between the Institute and an agency of the United States Government.
  - ○ (c) Agreements and transactions made or to be made by or through the Institute shall be subject to the same congressional notification, review, and approval requirements and procedures as if such agreements and transactions were made by or through the agency of the United States Government on behalf of which the Institute is acting.
  - ○ (d) During the two-year period beginning on the effective date of this Act, the Secretary of State shall transmit to the Speaker of the House and Senate House of Representatives and the Committee on Foreign Relations of Foreign Relations the Senate, every six months, a report describing and reviewing economic relations between the United States and Taiwan, noting any interference with normal commercial relations.

- RULES AND REGULATIONS
  - ○ SEC. 13. The President is authorized to prescribe such rules and regulations as he may deem appropriate to carry out the purposes of this Act. During the three-year period beginning on the effective date speaker of this Act, such rules and regulations shall be transmitted promptly to the Speaker of the House of Representatives and to the Committee on Foreign Relations of the Senate. Such action shall not, however, relieve the Institute of the responsibilities placed upon it by this Act.

- CONGRESSIONAL OVERSIGHT
  - ○ SEC. 14. (a) The Committee on Foreign Affairs of the House of Representatives, the Committee on Foreign Relations of the Senate, and other appropriate committees of the Congress shall monitor—
    - (1) the implementation of the provisions of this Act;
    - (2) the operation and procedures of the Institute;
    - (3) the legal and technical aspects of the continuing relationship between the United States and Taiwan; and
    - (4) the implementation of the policies of the United

States concerning security and cooperation in East Asia.

- o (b) Such committees shall report, as appropriate, to their respective Houses on the results of their monitoring

- DEFINITIONS
  - o SEC. 15. For purposes of this Act—
    - (1) the term "laws of the United States" includes any statute, rule, regulation, ordinance, order, or judicial rule of decision of the United States or any political subdivision thereof; and
    - (2) the term "Taiwan" includes, as the context may require, the islands of Taiwan and the Pescadores, the people on those islands, corporations and other entities and associations created or organized under the laws applied on those islands, and the governing authorities on Taiwan recognized by the United States as the Republic of China prior to January 1, 1979, and any successor governing authorities (including political subdivisions, agencies, and instrumentalities thereof).

- AUTHORIZATION OF APPROPRIATIONS
  - o SEC. 16. In addition to funds otherwise available to carry out the provisions of this Act, there are authorized to be appropriated to the Secretary of State for the fiscal year 1980 such funds as may be necessary to carry out such provisions. Such funds are authorized to remain available until expended.

- SEVERABILITY OF PROVISIONS
  - o SEC. 17. If any provision of this Act or the application thereof to any person or circumstance is held invalid, the remainder of the Act and the application of such provision to any other person or circumstance shall not be affected thereby.

- EFFECTIVE DATE
  - o SEC. 18. This Act shall be effective as of January 1, 1979. Approved April 10, 1979.

4. U.S.-PRC Joint Communiqué, August 17, 1982

1. In the Joint Communiqué on the Establishment of Diplomatic Relations on January 1, 1979, issued by the Government of the United States of America and the Government of the People's Republic of China, the United States of America recognized the Government of the People's Republic of China as the sole legal government of China, and it acknowledged the Chinese position that there is but one China and Taiwan is part of China. Within that context, the two sides agreed that the people of the United States would continue to maintain cultural, commercial, and other unofficial relations with the people of Taiwan. On this basis, relations between the United States and China were normalized.

2. The question of United States arms sales to Taiwan was not settled in the course of negotiations between the two countries on establishing diplomatic relations. The two sides held differing positions, and the Chinese side stated that it would raise the issue again following normalization. Recognizing that this issue would seriously hamper the development of United States-China relations, they have held further discussions on it, during and since the meetings between President Ronald Reagan and Premier Zhao Ziyang and between Secretary of State Alexander M. Haig, Jr., and Vice Premier and Foreign Minister Huang Hua in October 1981.

3. Respect for each other's sovereignty and territorial integrity and non-interference each other's internal affairs constitute the fundamental principles guiding United States-China relations. These principles were confirmed in the Shanghai Communiqué of February 28, 1972 and reaffirmed in the Joint Communiqué on the Establishment of Diplomatic Relations which came into effect on January 1, 1973.

Both sides emphatically state that these principles continue to govern all aspects of their relations.

4. The Chinese government reiterates that the question of Taiwan is China's internal affair. The Message to the Compatriots in Taiwan issued by China on January 1, 1979, promulgated a fundamental policy of striving for peaceful reunification of the Motherland. The Nine-Point Proposal put forward by China on September 30, 1981 represented a further major effort under this fundamental policy to strive for a peaceful solution to the Taiwan question.

5. The United States Government attaches great importance to its relations with China, and reiterates that it has no intention of infringing on Chinese sovereignty and territorial integrity, or interfering in China's internal affairs, or pursuing a policy of "two Chinas" or "one China, one Taiwan." The United States Government understands and appreciates the Chinese policy of striving for a peaceful resolution of the Taiwan question as indicated in China's Message to Compatriots in Taiwan issued on January 1, 1979 and the Nine-Point Proposal put forward by China on September 30, 1981. The new situation which has emerged with regard to the Taiwan question also provides favorable conditions for the settlement of United States-China differences over the question of United States arms sales to Taiwan.

6. Having in mind the foregoing statements of both sides, the United States Government states that it does not seek to carry out a long-term policy of arms sales to Taiwan, that its arms sales to Taiwan will not exceed, either in qualitative or in quantitative terms, the level of those supplied in recent years since the establishment of diplomatic relations between the United States and China, and that it intends to reduce gradually its sales of arms to Taiwan, leading over a period of time to a final resolution. In so stating, the United States acknowledges China's consistent position regarding the thorough settlement of this issue.

7. In order to bring about, over a period of time, a final settlement of the question of United States arms sales to Taiwan, which is an issue rooted in history, the two governments will make every effort to adopt measures and create conditions conducive to the thorough settlement of this issue.

8. The development of United States-China relations is not only in the interest of the two peoples but also conducive to peace and

stability in the world. The two sides are determined, on the principle of equality and mutual benefit, to strengthen their ties to the economic, cultural, educational, scientific, technological and other fields and make strong, joint efforts for the continued development of relations between the governments and peoples of the United States and China.

9. In order to bring about the healthy development of United States China relations, maintain world peace and oppose aggression and expansion, the two governments reaffirm the principles agreed on by the two sides in the Shanghai Communiqué and the Joint Communiqué on the Establishment of Diplomatic Relations. The two sides will maintain contact and hold appropriate consultations on bilateral and international issues of common interest.

5. Guidelines for National Unification, February 23, 1991

Adopted by the National Unification Council at its third meeting on February 23, 1991, and by the Executive Yuan Council at its 2223rd meeting on March 14, 1991.

The unification of China is meant to bring about a strong and prosperous nation with a long-lasting, bright future for its people; it is the common wish of Chinese people at home and abroad. After an appropriate period of forthright exchange, cooperation, and consultation conducted under the principles of reason, peace, parity, and reciprocity, the two sides of the Taiwan Straits should foster a consensus of democracy, freedom and equal prosperity, and together build a new and unified China. Based on this understanding, these Guidelines have been specially formulated with the express hope that all Chinese throughout the world will work with one mind toward their fulfillment.

To establish a democratic, free and equitably prosperous China.

1. Both the mainland and Taiwan areas are parts of Chinese territory. Helping to bring about national unification should be the common responsibility of all Chinese people.

2. The unification of China should be for the welfare of all its people and not be subject to partisan conflict.

3. China's unification should aim at promoting Chinese culture, safeguarding human dignity, guaranteeing fundamental human rights, and practicing democracy and the rule of law.

4. The timing and manner of China's unification should first respect the rights and interests of the people in the Taiwan area, and protect their security and welfare. It should be achieved in gradual phases under the principles of reason, peace, parity, and reciprocity.

1. Short term—A phase of exchanges and reciprocity.

(1) To enhance understanding through exchanges between the two sides of the Straits and eliminate hostility through reciprocity; and to establish a mutually benign relationship by not endangering each other's security and stability while in the midst of exchanges and not denying the other's existence as a political entity while in the midst of effecting reciprocity.

(2) To set up an order for exchanges across the Straits, to draw up regulations for such exchanges, and to establish intermediary organizations so as to protect people's rights and interest on both sides of the Straits; to gradually ease various restrictions and expand people-to-people contacts so as to promote the social prosperity of both sides.

(3) In order to improve the people's welfare on both sides of the Straits with the ultimate objective of unifying the nation, in the mainland area economic reform should be carried out forthrightly, the expression of public opinion there should gradually be allowed, and both democracy and the rule of law should be implemented; while in the Taiwan area efforts should be made to accelerate constitutional reform and promote national development to establish a society of equitable prosperity.

(4) The two sides of the Straits should end the state of hostility and, under the *principle of one China,* solve all disputes through peaceful means, and furthermore respect—not reject—each other in the international community, so as to move toward a phase of mutual trust and cooperation.

2. Medium Term—A phase of mutual trust and cooperation.

(1) Both sides of the Straits should establish official communication channels on equal footing.

(2) Direct postal, transport and commercial links should be allowed, and both sides should jointly develop the southeastern coastal area of Chinese mainland and then gradually extend this development to other areas of the mainland in order to narrow the gap in living standards between the two sides.

(3) Both sides of the Straits should work together and assist each other in taking part in international organizations and activities.

(4) Mutual visits by high-ranking officials on both sides should be

promoted to create favorable conditions for consultation and unification.

3. Long term—A phase of consultation and unification.

A consultative organization for unification should be established through which both sides, in accordance with the will of the people in both the mainland and Taiwan areas, and while adhering to the goals of democracy, economic freedom, social justice and nationalization of the armed forces, jointly discuss the grand task of unification and map out a constitutional system to establish a democratic, free, and equitably prosperous China.

6. Continue to Promote the Reunification of China (The Eight-Point Policy by Jiang Zemin), January 30, 1995

(On January 30, 1995, at a New Year tea party given by the Taiwan Affaires Offices under the Central Committee of CPC and the State Council, President Jiang Zemin delivered a speech entitled "Continue to Promote the Reunification of China." He stated his views and eight propositions on a number of important questions that have a bearing on the development of relations between the two sides and the promotion of a peaceful reunification of the motherland.)

Comrades and friends:

Following the celebration of the 1995 New Year's Day, people of all ethnic groups in China are now greeting the Spring Festival. On the occasion of this traditional festival of the Chinese nation, it is of great significance for Taiwan compatriots in Beijing and other related personages to gather here to discuss the future of relations between the two sides of the Taiwan Straits and the peaceful reunification of our motherland. On behalf of the Central Committee of the Communist Party of China and the State Council, I would like to take this opportunity to wish our 21 million compatriots in Taiwan a happy New Year and the best of Luck.

Taiwan is an integral part of China. A hundred years ago, on April 17, 1895, the Japanese imperialist, by waging a war against the corrupt government of the Qing Dynasty, forced it to sign the Shimoneseki Treaty of national betrayal and humiliation. Under the treaty, Japan seized Taiwan and the Penghu Islands, subjecting the people of Taiwan to its colonial rule for half a century. The Chinese people will never forget this humiliating chapter of our history. Fifty years ago, together with the people of other countries, the Chinese people defeated the Japanese imperialists. October 15, 1945 saw the return of of Taiwan and the Penghu Islands to China and marked the end of Japan's colonial rule over our compatriots in Taiwan. However, for reasons known to all, Taiwan has been severed from the Chinese mainland since 1949. It remains the inviolable mission and lofty goal fo the Chinese people to achieve the reunification of their motherland and promote an all-round revitalization of the nation.

Since the Standing Committee of the National People's Congress issued its "Message to the Taiwan Compatriots" in January 1979, we have formulated the basic principles of peaceful reunification and "one country, two systems" and a series of policies towards Taiwan. Comrade Deng Xiaoping, the chief architect of China's reform and opening to the outside world, is also the inventor of the great concept of "one country, two systems." With foresight and seeking truth from facts, he put forward a series of important theories and ideas concerning the settlement of the Taiwan question that reflect distinct features of the times and defined guiding principles for a peaceful reunification of the motherland.

Comrade Deng Xiaoping has pointed out that the core of the issue is the reunification of the motherland. All descendants of the Chinese nation wish to see China reunified. It is against the will of the nation to see it divided. There is only one China, and Taiwan is a part of China. We will never allow there to be "two Chinas" or "one China, one Taiwan." There are only two ways to settle the Taiwan questions: one is by peaceful means and the other is by non-peaceful means. The way the Taiwan question is to be settled is China's internal affair and brooks no foreign interference. We consistently stand for achieving reunification by peaceful means and through negotiations. But we will not undertake not to use force. Such commitment would only make it impossible to achieve a peaceful reunification and could only lead to the eventual settlement of the question by the use of force.

After Taiwan is reunified with the mainland, China will pursue the policy of "one country, two systems." The main part of the country will adhere to the socialist system, while Taiwan will retain its current system. "Reunification does not mean that the mainland will swallow up Taiwan, nor does it mean that Taiwan will swallow up the mainland." After Taiwan's reunification with the mainland, its social and economic systems will not change, nor will its way of life and its non-governmental relations with foreign countries. This means that foreign investments in Taiwan and non-governmental exchanges between Taiwan and other countries will not be affected.

As a special administrative region, Taiwan will exercise a high degree of autonomy and enjoy legislative and independent judicial power, including that of final adjudication. It may also retain its armed forces and administer its party, governmental and military systems by itself. The central government will not station troops or send administrative personnel there. What is more, a number of posts in the central government will be made available to Taiwan.

The past decade and more has witnessed a vigorous expansion in cross-strait visits by individuals and exchanges in science, technology, culture, academic affairs, sports and other fields under the guidance of the basic principle of peaceful reunification and "one country, two systems," and through the concerted efforts of compatriots on both sides of the Taiwan Straits and in Hong Kong and Macao and Chinese residing abroad.

A situation in which the economies of the two sides promote, complement and benefit each other is taking shape. Establishment of direct links between the two sides for postal, air and shipping services and trade at an early date not only represents the strong desire of vast numbers of compatriots in Taiwan, particularly industrialist and businessmen, but has also become an actual requirement for future economic development in Taiwan. Progress has been registered in negotiations on specific issues, and the "Wang Daohan-Koo Chenfu talks" represent an important historic step forward in relations between the two sides.

However, what the Chinese people should watch out for is the growing separatist tendency and the increasingly rampant activities of forces on the island working for the "independence of Taiwan" in recent years. Certain foreign forces have further meddled in the issue of Taiwan, interfering in China's internal affairs. All this not only impedes the process of China's peaceful reunification, but also threatens peace, stability and development in the Asia-Pacific region.

The current international situation is still complex and volatile, but in general it is moving towards relaxation. All countries in the world are working out their economic strategies for the future and regard it as a task of primary importance to increase their overall national strength so as to take up their proper places in the world in the next century. We are pleased to see that the economies of both sides are growing. In 1997 and 1999, China resumed the exercise of sovereignty over Hong Kong and Macao respectively, which will be happy events for the Chinese of all ethnic groups, including our compatriots in Taiwan.

The Chinese nation has experienced many vicissitudes and hardships, and now is high time to accomplish reunification of the motherland and revitalize the nation. This means an opportunity for Taiwan; it also means an opportunity for the entire Chinese nation. Here, I would like to state the following views and propositions on a number of important questions that have a bearing on the development of relations between the two sides and the promotion of a peaceful reunification of the motherland.

1. Adherence to the principle of one China is the basis and premise for peaceful reunification. China's sovereignty and territory must never be allowed to suffer division. We must firmly oppose any words or actions aimed at creating the "independence of Taiwan" and propositions that run counter to the principle of one China such as "two split sides with separate administrations," "two Chinas over a period of time" and so on.

2. We do not challenge development of non-governmental economic and cultural ties by Taiwan with other countries. Under the principle of one China and in accordance with the charters of relevant international organizations, Taiwan has become a member of the Asian Development Bank, the Asia-Pacific Economic Cooperation Forum and other international economic organizations in the name of "Chinese Taipei." However, we oppose Taiwan's activities in "expanding" its "international living space" which aim to create "two Chinas" or "one China, one Taiwan." All patriotic compatriots in Taiwan and other people of insight understand that, instead of solving problems, such activities can only help forces working for the "independence of Taiwan" undermine the process of peaceful reunification. Only after peaceful reunification is accomplished can Taiwan compatriots truly and fully share the international dignity and honor attained by our great motherland with other Chinese.

3. It has been our consistent stand to hold negotiations with the Taiwan authorities on the peaceful reunification of the motherland.

Representatives from various political parties and mass organizations on both sides of the Taiwan Straits can be invited to participate in such talks. I said in my report at the 14th National Congress of the Communist Party of China held in October 1992, "On the premise that there is only one China, we are prepared to talk with the Taiwan authorities about any matter, including the form that official negotiations should take, a form that would be acceptable to both sides;" "on the premise that there is only one China, we are prepared to talk with the Taiwan authorities about any matter," we mean, naturally, that all matters of concern to the Taiwan authorities are included. We have proposed time and again that negotiations should be held on officially ending the state of hostility between the two sides and accomplishing peaceful reunification in a step-by-step way. Here again I solemnly proposed that such negotiations be held. I suggest that, as the first step, negotiations should be held and an agreement reached on officially ending the state of hostility between the two sides in accordance with the principle that there is only one China. On the basis, the two sides should undertake jointly to safeguard China's sovereignty and territorial integrity and map our plans for the future development of their relations. As for the name, place and form of such political talks, a solution acceptable to both sides can certainly be found so long as consultations on an equal footing can be held at an early date.

4. We should strive for a peaceful reunification of the motherland since Chinese should not fight Chinese. Our not undertaking to give up the use of forces is not directed against our compatriots in Taiwan, but against the schemes of foreign forces to interfere with China's reunification and to bring about the "independence of Taiwan. We are fully confident that our compatriots in Taiwan, Hong Kong and Macao and all Chinese residing overseas would understand this principled position of ours.

5. In face of the development of the world economy in the 21st century, great efforts should be made to expand economic exchanges and cooperation between the two sides so as to achieve prosperity for both to the benefit of the entire nation. We maintain that political differences should not affect or interfere with economic cooperation between the two sides. We will continue to implement over a long period of time the policy of encouraging industrialists and business-

men from Taiwan to invest in the mainland and enforce Law of the People's Republic of China for Protecting Investments of Taiwan Compatriots. We will safeguard the legitimate rights and interests of industrialists and businessmen from Taiwan under whatever circumstances. We should continue to expand contacts and exchanges between our compatriots on both sides so as to increase mutual understanding and trust. Since direct links for postal, air and shipping services and trade between the two sides are an objective requirement for their economic development and contacts in various fields, and since such links serve the interests of people on both sides, it is absolutely necessary to adopt practical measures to speed up the establishment of such direct links. Efforts should be made to promote negotiations on specific issues between the two sides. We are in favor of conducting this kind of negotiations on the basis of reciprocity and mutual benefit and signing non-governmental agreements on the protection of the rights and interests of industrialists and businessmen from Taiwan.

6. The splendid culture of 5,000 years created by the sons and daughters of all ethnic groups of China has become times that keep the entire Chinese people close at heart. It constitutes an important basis for a peaceful reunification of the motherland. People on both sides of the Taiwan Straits should jointly inherit and carry forward the fine traditions of Chinese culture.

7. The 21 million compatriots in Taiwan, whether born there or from other provinces, are all Chinese. They are our own flesh and blood. We should fully respect their life style and their wish to be the masters of their own destiny and protect all their legitimate rights and interests. Relevant departments of our government including agencies stationed abroad should strengthen contacts with compatriots from Taiwan, listen to their views and wishes, care for and look after their interests and make every effort to help them solve their problems. We hope Taiwan Island enjoys social stability, economic growth and a high living standard. We also hope all political parties in Taiwan will adopt a sensible, forward-looking and constructive attitude and promote the expansion of relations between the two sides. All parties and personages of all circles in Taiwan are welcome to exchange views with us on relations between the two sides and on peaceful reunification. They are also welcome to visit and tour the mainland.

History will remember the deeds of all personages from various circles who contribute to the reunification of China.

8. Leaders of the Taiwan authorities are welcome to visit the mainland in appropriate capacities. We are also ready to accept invitations to visit Taiwan. The two sides can discuss state affairs or exchange ideas on some questions first. Even a simple visit to the other side will be useful. The affairs of the Chinese people should be handled by Chinese themselves, something that does not take an international occasion to accomplish. The Taiwan Straits is narrow and people on both sides eagerly look forward to meeting each other. They should exchange visits instead of being kept from seeing each other all their lives.

Our compatriots in Hong Kong and Macao and all Chinese residing abroad have made dedicated efforts to promote closer relations between the two sides, the reunification of the motherland and revitalization of the nation. Their contributions will always be remembered. We hope they will make new contributions in this regard.

Reunification of the motherland is the common aspiration of the Chinese people. All patriotic compatriots do not wish to see reunification delayed indefinitely. Dr. Sun Yat-sen, the great revolutionary forerunner of the Chinese nation, once said "Reunification is the hope of all people of the Chinese nation. Reunification, and all people of the country will enjoy a happy life; failure to accomplish reunification, and they will suffer." We appeal to all Chinese to unite and hold high the great banner of patriotism, uphold reunification, oppose secession, spare no effort in promoting the expansion of relations between the two sides and work for the accomplishment of China's reunification. The glorious day of reunification is sure to arrive in the course of modern development of the Chinese nation.

7. Anti-Secession Law, March 2005

(Adopted at the Third Session of the 10th National People's Congress on March 14, 2005)

Article 1   This Law is formulated, in accordance with the Constitution, for the purpose of opposing and checking Taiwan's secession from China by secessionists in the name of "Taiwan independence," promoting peaceful national reunification, maintaining peace and stability in the Taiwan Straits, preserving China's sovereignty and territorial integrity, and safeguarding the fundamental interests of the Chinese nation.

Article 2   There is only one China in the world. Both the mainland and Taiwan belong to one China. China's sovereignty and territorial integrity brook no division. Safeguarding China's sovereignty and territorial integrity is the common obligation of all Chinese people, the Taiwan compatriots included.

Taiwan is part of China. The State shall never allow the "Taiwan independence" secessionist forces to make Taiwan secede from China under any name or by any means.

Article 3   The Taiwan question is one that is left over from China's civil war of the late 1940s.

Solving the Taiwan question and achieving national reunification is China's internal affair, which subjects to no interference by any outside forces.

Article 4   Accomplishing the great task of reunifying the motherland is the sacred duty of all Chinese people, the Taiwan compatriots included.

Article 5 Upholding the principle of one China is the basis of peaceful reunification of the country.

To reunify the country through peaceful means best serves the fundamental interests of the compatriots on both sides of the Taiwan Straits. The State shall do its utmost with maximum sincerity to achieve a peaceful reunification.

After the country is reunified peacefully, Taiwan may practice systems different from those on the mainland and enjoy a high degree of autonomy.

Article 6 The State shall take the following measures to maintain peace and stability in the Taiwan Straits and promote cross-Straits relations:

(1) to encourage and facilitate personnel exchanges across the Straits for greater mutual understanding and mutual trust;

(2) to encourage and facilitate economic exchanges and co-operation, realize direct links of trade, mail and air and shipping services, and bring about closer economic ties between the two sides of the Straits to their mutual benefit;

(3) to encourage and facilitate cross-Straits exchanges in education, science, technology, culture, health and sports, and work together to carry forward the proud Chinese cultural traditions;

(4) to encourage and facilitate cross-Straits co-operation in combating crimes; and

(5) to encourage and facilitate other activities that are conducive to peace and stability in the Taiwan Straits and stronger cross-Straits relations.

The State protects the rights and interests of the Taiwan compatriots in accordance with law.

Article 7 The State stands for the achievement of peaceful reunification through consultations and negotiations on an equal footing between the two sides of the Taiwan Straits. These consultations and negotiations may be conducted in steps and phases and with flexible and varied modalities.

The two sides of the Taiwan Straits may consult and negotiate on the following matters:

(1) officially ending the state of hostility between the two sides;

(2) mapping out the development of cross-Straits relations;

(3) steps and arrangements for peaceful national reunification;

(4) the political status of the Taiwan authorities;

(5) the Taiwan region's room of international operation that is compatible with its status; and

(6) other matters concerning the achievement of peaceful national reunification.

Article 8   In the event that the "Taiwan independence" secessionist forces should act under any name or by any means to cause the fact of Taiwan's secession from China, or that major incidents entailing Taiwan's secession from China should occur, or that possibilities for a peaceful reunification should be completely exhausted, the state shall employ non-peaceful means and other necessary measures to protect China's sovereignty and territorial integrity.

The State Council and the Central Military Commission shall decide on and execute the non-peaceful means and other necessary measures as provided for in the preceding paragraph and shall promptly report to the Standing Committee of the National People's Congress.

Article 9   In the event of employing and executing non-peaceful means and other necessary measures as provided for in this Law, the State shall exert its utmost to protect the lives, property and other legitimate rights and interests of Taiwan civilians and foreign nationals in Taiwan, and to minimize losses. At the same time, the State shall protect the rights and interests of the Taiwan compatriots in other parts of China in accordance with law.

Article 10   This Law shall come into force on the day of its promulgation.

About the Authors

Ramon H. Myers is senior fellow at the Hoover Institution, Stanford University. He is the coauthor of *The First Chinese Democracy: Political Life in the Republic of China on Taiwan* (Johns Hopkins University Press, 1998) and author of numerous articles about Taiwan's political and economic history. His most recent publication, as coeditor with Michel Oksenberg and David L. Shambaugh, is *Making China Policy: Lessons from the Bush and Clinton Administrations* (Rowman & Littlefield, 2001).

Jialin Zhang is a visiting scholar at the Hoover Institution. He received his degree at the Moscow Institute of International Relations in 1960 and served as a senior fellow at the Shanghai Institute for International Studies. He is the author of several Hoover Institution essays: *China's Response to the Downfall of Communism in Eastern Europe and the Soviet Union* (1994), *An Assessment of Chinese Thinking on Trade Liberalization* (1997), *U.S.-China Trade Issues after the WTO and the PNTR Deal—a Chinese Perspective* (2000), and *The Debate on China's Exchange Rate—Should or Will It Be Revalued?* (2004). He is also the coauthor of *The Turnover of Political Power in Taiwan* (2002).

Index

Acheson, Dean, 2–3
Act for Promoting Mandarin, 60
Act of Local Institutions, 59
ADB. *See* Asian Development
    Bank
Airis, 73
AIT. *See* American Institute on
    Taiwan
The Alliance to Campaign for
    Rectifying the Name of Taiwan,
    97
A-Mei. *See* Chang Hui-mei
American Institute on Taiwan, 64,
    73, 135–40
Anti-Secession Law, 156–58;
    military force conditions set by,
    106; passing of, 106; response
    to, 105
ARATS. *See* Association for
    Relations Across the Taiwan
    Strait
Asian Development Bank (ADB),
    18–19, 152
Asia-Pacific Economic Community,
    34, 152
assassination attempt, 92–93
Association for Relations Across
    the Taiwan Strait (ARATS), 22,
    24, 38, 40, 80; meetings with

SEF, 29, 34; negotiations with
    SEF, 25; "one China" principle
    demanded by, 25; oral
    statement on "one China," 26
Singapore meeting with SEF, 27.
    See also People's Republic of
    China (PRC)
"avoiding haste by being patient"
    policy, 37, 42, 72

bensheng ren (Taiwan natives), 48
Bush, George W., 88

Cathay Pacific Airways, 19
Caucus for Strengthening ROC
    Sovereign Nation Status, 41–42
CCP. *See* Chinese Communist
    Party
Chang Hui-mei, 97
Chen Shimong, 66
Chen Shui-bian, 58, 61, 78, 82,
    83, 102–3, 105, 115; on Anti-
    Secession Law, 105, 107;
    assassination attempt on, 92–
    93; China criticized by, 98; DPP
    chairmanship resigned from by,
    99–100; economic conference
    sponsored by, 70; economic
    initiatives by, 83; economic
    policy changes by, 72; election